ORCS & GOBLINS

CONTENTS

By Matthew Ward

Additional Material: Andy Hoare. **Original Book:** Rick Priestley. **Cover Art:** Alex Boyd. **Illustration:** John Blanche, Alex Boyd, Paul Dainton, David Gallagher, Paul Jeacock, Karl Kopinski & Adrian Smith. **Graphic Design:** Alun Davies & Nathan Winter. **Miniatures Sculptors:** Tim Adcock, Mike Anderson, Alex Hedström, Trish Morrison, Brian Nelson, Seb Perbet, Steve Saleh & Dave Thomas. **'Eavy Metal:** Fil Dunn, Pete Foley, Neil Green, Neil Langdown, Darren Latham, Keith Robertson, Anja Wettergren & Kirsten Williams. **Hobby Material:** Dave Andrews, Mark Jones, Chad Mierzwa, Dominic Murray & Adrian Wood. **Production:** Michelle Barson, Chris Eggar, Marc Elliott, Dylan Owen, Mark Owen & Ian Strickland. **Thanks To:** Peter Borlace, Alessio Cavatore, Graham Davey, Alan Merrett, Rick Priestley, Gavin Thorpe, Jeremy Vetock & The Geeks play-testers.

Produced by Games Workshop

British Cataloguing-in-Publication Data. A catalogue record for this book is available from the British Library.

Pictures are used for illustrative purposes only. Certain Citadel products may be dangerous if used incorrectly and Games Workshop does not recommend them for use by children under the age of 16 without adult supervision. Whatever your age, be careful when using glues, bladed equipment and sprays and make sure that you read and follow the instructions on the packaging.

UK	US	Canada	Australia	Northern Europe
Games Workshop Ltd., Willow Rd, Lenton, Nottingham. NG7 2WS	Games Workshop Inc., 6711 Baymeadow Drive, Glen Burnie, Maryland 21060-6401	Games Workshop, 2679 Bristol Circle, Unit 3, Oakville, Ontario, L6H 6Z8	Games Workshop, 23 Liverpool Street, Ingleburn NSW 2565	Games Workshop Ltd., Willow Rd, Lenton, Nottingham. NG7 2WS UK

ISBN: 1-84154-785-9   www.games-workshop.com   Product code: 60 03 02 09 003

INTRODUCTION

If you are looking for a fight, you've found it! The Orcs and Goblins are brutal but cunning green-skinned warriors whose only goal is to rampage and slaughter. This book is the definitive guide to collecting, painting and playing with an Orcs & Goblins army for the game of Warhammer.

THE WARHAMMER GAME

The Warhammer rulebook contains the rules you need to fight battles with your Citadel miniatures. Every army has its own book that works with these rules and allows you to turn your collection of miniatures into an organised force, ready for battle. This particular 'Army book' describes the warlike Orcs and Goblins, their army list and the miniatures you can collect.

WHY COLLECT AN ORCS & GOBLINS ARMY?

Orcs are quarrelsome, angry creatures, capable of pounding any opponent to bloody scraps. But beware – if there are no enemies around they will soon start hitting each other! You'll cheer as your mighty green-skinned warriors crush all before them. You'll bellow with rage as your army grinds to a squabbling halt. Whatever happens, dere's gonna be sum fightin'…

An Orcs & Goblins army will often contain a vast array of different troop types, from the wide variety of greenskins themselves, to monstrous beasts such as Trolls, Giants and Giant Spiders. Whilst Orcs prefer to hurl themselves into close combat as swiftly as possible, Goblins bring a lethal array of sneakiness, such as foolhardy Doom Diver Catapults and mushroom-fuelled Night Goblin Fanatics. You can choose an elite army of hard-hitting Orcs, or go for a massive horde full of Goblins – or anything in-between!

HOW THIS BOOK WORKS

Every Army book is split into four main sections that deal with different aspects of the army. Warhammer Armies: Orcs & Goblins contains:

Greenskins. The first section introduces the ferocious greenskins and their deeds in the Warhammer world. It covers the most powerful leaders of the Orcs and Goblins and the bloody swathes of destruction they have caused.

Bestiary. Each and every unit type, monster, hero and war machine in the Orcs & Goblins army is examined in the bestiary. You will find a full description, alongside complete rules and details of any unique abilities they possess.

Army List. The army list takes all of the warriors presented in the previous section and arranges them so you can choose an army for your games.

The Orcs & Goblins Army. The final section contains photographs of the Citadel miniatures that make up the Orcs & Goblins army. Colour schemes for the different tribes and example armies can all be found in this section.

FIND OUT MORE

While Warhammer Armies: Orcs & Goblins contains everything you need to play a game with your army, there are always more tactics to use, different battles to fight and painting ideas to try out. The monthly magazine White Dwarf contains articles about all aspects of the Warhammer game and hobby, and you can find articles specific to the Orcs and Goblins on our website:

www.games-workshop.com

GREENSKINS

Orcs live to fight. For an Orc there is no greater joy than to be in the thick of a battle, where the biggest and meanest warrior carries the day. Such belligerence is both a strength and a weakness as it means that Orcs expend much of their energy fighting amongst themselves, rather than against a slightly more distant foe.

Orcish skin is tougher than hide leather and curiously waxy. As an Orc ages, its skin becomes scabby, gnarled and even more impenetrable, to the point where the most determined sword stroke can cause only a scratch. If the skin is pierced and the purplish-red blood begins to flow, there is no guarantee that the wound will prevent the Orc from pulverising his opponent. Orcs are capable of healing at an incredible pace. If an Orc's severed arm is stitched back into place, however crudely, it will heal back as good as new within days. Orcs naturally take their robust bodies for granted and regard everyone else as weak, fragile and 'squishy'.

Smaller and more nimble than their Orcish cousins, Goblins have a more developed sense of self-preservation. They are cunning rather than strong, and tend to leave the serious business of fighting to the Orcs. Goblins prefer to guard the rear of an army, though in desperate circumstances they'll finish off an enemy so long as it has been given a clobbering by a mob of Orcs. Nevertheless, Goblin raiding parties are rightly feared on the edges of the more civilised lands. When they attack, Goblins generally either have numbers on their side or something larger and meaner giving them orders.

There are many varied subspecies of greenskin. Night Goblins live in the deepest caves, venturing out into the light of the sun only when suitably fortified by fungus beer. Forest Goblins prowl the gloomy forests of the Empire, and Southland jungle canopies reverberate to the steady pounding of Savage Orc drums. Most notable and fearsome of all, Black Orcs are 'ard as nails, and inevitably take over any tribe they join, leaving a trail of butchered and dismembered rivals in their wake.

WARBOSSES

Greenskin tribes are led by a Warboss – the biggest and loudest Orc – with the other greenskins following out of both respect and a desire to avoid a pummelling for not following. A tribe's success is highly reliant upon just how hard their Warboss can wallop things. Warbosses rarely command great loyalty from their followers – although a chieftain

may be admired for his ability to push an opponent's nose through his brainpan. Greenskins are not sentimental creatures – they may remember a great leader but they certainly won't mourn him. Upon a Warboss' death, whether in battle or out of it, leadership swiftly and inevitably falls to the next biggest and loudest Orc in the immediate vicinity. At the battle of Doom Mountain, Nagrat Headsplitter's corpse had barely touched the ground before his second in command began clubbing the Dwarf king with Nagrat's own – still twitching – severed arm.

A Warboss will also inevitably face challenges from within his own ranks – especially if the fightin' and lootin' hasn't been so good lately. For Orcs, such challenges are typically direct and involve a large bladed or blunt implement (which can be a handy Goblin, in desperate circumstances). Being smaller and possessed of a quite remarkable cowardice, Goblins are rather more circumspect in their challenges. The mantle of Goblin Warboss can be won in a direct challenge, but other methods are often preferred. The defences set in place by the leader of the Backstabbas tribe, Ratgut the Ragged, (which included a suit of heavy chainmail and the habit of having his back to the wall at all times) were to no avail – he exploded in a shower of pungent ichor after eating a dish of edible mushrooms that mysteriously turned out to be inedible mushrooms.

THE DOMINION OF THE ORCS

Orcs don't have kingdoms or countries in the same way as Men, but there are nevertheless areas where Orcs or Goblins are very definitely in control. Most Orcs see the world as being split into two types of land: 'green' and 'da uvver bits'. A more ambitious Warboss will see things in more detail: 'my green', 'green wot is gonna be mine' and 'da uvver bits'.

Orcs and Goblins are far more numerous in the Badlands, and in some places they are the dominant (nearly) intelligent creature. Those areas that are not complete wasteland before the arrival of Orcs are trampled into desolation shortly after. This, combined with the unquenchable Orc bloodlust, often makes tribes nomadic in nature, though greenskins will stay put for a time once they've captured a particularly large and defensible fortress. That said, even a settled tribe can leave its fortifications when a Waaagh! is called.

THE POWER OF THE WAAAGH!

Commonly, a warband will sweep into a village, slaughter the inhabitants and charge on, pausing just long enough for the warlord to make a really big pile of severed heads to sit on. Terrifying and brutal as this is, it is when a Waaagh! is called that the Orcs become a truly dangerous force.

A Waaagh! is akin to a migrating invasion, when some successful Warboss throws everything he's got against his chosen enemy and all the other Orcs and Goblins flock to join him.

A Waaagh! is truly a sight to freeze the blood – an unstoppable sea of green-skinned monsters swarming across the horizon, whooping, jeering, and yelling their barbarous war cries.

The nature of the Waaagh! means that the history of Orcs and Goblins, as passed down by word of mouth through the tribes, is rather fragmented. Greenskin history is generally an account of the rise and fall of huge Waaagh!s and their glorious leaders. Other campaigns involving the Orcs and Goblins do feature in the histories of other races, such as Sigmar's campaigns that led to the Battle of Black Fire Pass, and the travails of Gilles the Breton in the forming of the realm of Bretonnia, but the Orcs make little to no effort to remember these – chiefly because they lost to 'da squishy 'umies'.

ORC HISTORY

The history of the Orcs and Goblins, as recorded by Men, Elves and Dwarfs, is an account of the rise and fall of huge tribes that have fought against them. Only the really big and powerful tribes impinge upon Human or Dwarf history. As such it is a fragmented – but spectacularly bloody – account, punctuated by occasions when the whole of the Old World stood on the brink of destruction.

WAAAGH! GORBAD

Gorbad Ironclaw was one of the most feared Orc leaders of all time. His campaign of destruction raged across the Empire and left the region of Solland so devastated that it never recovered.

Gorbad's tribe, the Ironclaw Orcs, lived around the Iron Rock for many years, and their fortunes rose and fell as is the way of Orc tribes. The chief rival of the Ironclaws was the Broken Tooth tribe – until Gorbad led a surprise attack through the ancient Dwarf tunnels and forcibly deposed the Broken Tooth's chieftain, the notoriously huge and brutal Crusher Zogoth.

In the aftermath of Gorbad's victory, the Broken Tooths readily accepted Gorbad as their new leader, as is the fashion of Orcs who know when they are beaten and who would much sooner be on the winning side. With the Broken Tooths under his clawed thumb, Gorbad soon conquered the surrounding Goblin and Night Goblin tribes and vastly increased the size, if not the discipline, of the army at his command. Waaagh! Gorbad had begun. The Waaagh! rapidly gained in strength as it headed towards Black Fire Pass, with dozens of Goblin tribes flocking to its banner.

Gorbad's army poured from the mountains, following the old Dwarf road down to the Empire. Seemingly unstoppable, the Waaagh! looted and destroyed the Moot, and razed the towns of Averheim and Nuln in short order. The destruction of Nuln was a great blow to the Emperor Sigismund and a mighty victory for Gorbad, for the armies of the Empire began to lose their resolve whilst Gorbad's numbers increased daily.

THE BATTLE OF SOLLAND'S CROWN

In a matter of weeks the whole of Solland and Wissenland were plundered and burned. Count Eldred of Solland was hacked down by Gorbad's axe, Morglor the Mangler, and the Elector's ancestral Runefang was taken as a trophy even as his banner was trampled into the mud. According to legend, Gorbad tore the crown of Solland from the Count's head and perched it upon his own, sporting it thereafter as a token of his victory.

Days later, the Count of Wissenland achieved a little more, lancing his blade deep into Gorbad's chest, but lost his sword arm to the Orc's vengeful counter-attack. Only a desperate charge by the Wissenland Greatswords managed to hold Gorbad at bay whilst the Count's horse dragged its master's bloody figure from the field. Driven into a rage by his wound, Gorbad swiftly put the Greatswords to flight. For weeks following the battle, the Orcs rampaged through the southern regions of the Empire, burning and looting, until surging northwards once again, towards Altdorf.

THE SIEGE OF ALTDORF

In Altdorf, the elected Emperor Sigismund prepared for the Orc invasion by fortifying the city's walls and gathering in the harvests. The greenskins swiftly began quarrelling over what little supplies could be found until Gorbad, given sour humour by his wound, settled the dispute by decapitating the ringleaders (and a few nearby Goblins, for good measure). Determined not to give his followers a chance to begin squabbling anew, Gorbad launched straight into an attack on Altdorf's walls – an ill-prepared assault that was bloodily repelled.

Impatient with the delay, Gorbad bellowed his Warbosses into another attack. Unfortunately, the marshes around Altdorf made it difficult for the Orcs. Hundreds of greenskins were choked and drowned as they stomped through the muddy fens when a violent argument broke out over the correct path through the morass.

Seeing the chaos before him, Gorbad had no choice but to halt the attack and prepare for a long siege. At first his rock lobbers pounded the walls and bombarded the city with huge boulders, destroying bastions and pummelling buildings to powder. In response, the city's cannons trained their fire against the rock lobbers, reducing them to scraps of timber in short order. Gorbad, still unable to breach Altdorf's walls, decided to unleash his secret weapon and severed the chains on several great wagons that had been hauled down from the mountains. With an ear-shattering roar – and a bowel-churning stench – a half-dozen mighty wyverns burst free from their dank cages and swept upwards towards Altdorf. The ill-tempered beasts swooped and dived on the city's guardians, their vicious claws tearing men asunder and unseating cannons with ease.

Amongst the commotion, one of the wyverns swept inside the Emperor's palace, ripping through the roof of the great hall. For several hours the wyvern rampaged through the Imperial palace, eating servants by the dozen and dunging in the banqueting hall. Every time the defenders attempted to block the lizard's progress it would merely shoulder its way through another wall in a shower of wooden splinters and brick dust.

When Sigismund led a group of archers against the beast, it just brushed the bowmen aside with one mighty sweep of its tail and seized the Emperor in its foetid jaws. Imperial records describe how the surviving archers fled from the wet snapping sounds that swiftly followed, although some reports describe a second wyvern battling the first for the regal remains. With its appetite temporarily sated, the wyvern made a nest of banners and tapestries in the throne room. As it started to slumber, a cadre of furious knights burst in and took bloody revenge for their Emperor.

Elsewhere in the city, the Supreme Patriarch of the Colleges of Magic slew a wyvern in a burst of eldritch fire, and another was slain in the explosion of a malfunctioning volley gun. With a good portion of Gorbad's secret strategy either dead or in well-fed and contented slumbers, his army could do little other than sit and stare at the city walls. True to form, the wyvern attack had ignored Altdorf's gates, despite painstaking instructions to the contrary.

As time ebbed away the magical wound inflicted by the Count of Wissenland began to trouble Gorbad more with each passing day. Gorbad began to rage in fevered pain, bellowing at his minions and cursing his underlings for failing to deliver Altdorf. Gradually Gorbad's Waaagh! dissipated and the tribes returned to the forests and mountains. Eventually even Gorbad had to give up, and he turned his back on the smouldering and battle-scarred city of Altdorf.

THE WAAAGH! COLLAPSES

The Ironclaws and the Broken Tooths were all that was left of the countless greenskin tribes that had flocked to Gorbad's banner. Gorbad Ironclaw withdrew to the east, following the River Reik back to the Worlds Edge Mountains. As his depleted army made its way home it was harried by the forces of a vengeful Empire, and even attacked by Orc tribes that had once fought as part of the Waaagh! There was to be only one more major battle, the Battle of Blood Peak, fought in the shadow of the notorious red-coloured mountain south of Black Fire Pass. It was here that the still formidable remainder of the

Orc horde was confronted by a Dwarf army led by the King of Karaz-a-Karak. During his first march into the west Gorbad had broken into many Dwarf tombs, an act of desecration that the stunties had not forgotten. Though Gorbad stood firm against the Dwarfen fury, his army began to crumble around him. As dusk came down, Gorbad was knee-deep in defeated foes, his mighty axe visiting bloody ruin on all about him, roaring defiance even as the Dwarfs surrounded him.

Gorbad was never again seen in the lands of the Empire. As Orcs keep few records of any kind it is uncertain as to whether or not Gorbad was slain in that final great battle – if the Dwarfs can confirm his fate, they're not saying. Perhaps he escaped, regained his old power in the Badlands and rebuilt his domain. Whatever became of Gorbad, his reputation and memory live on. To Orcs, he has become a great hero who stands beside the gods Gork and Mork. To Men, he is a reminder of the terrifying destructive power of the Waaagh!

WAAAGH! GROM

Most of the warlords whose campaigns of annihilation have shaken the world have been Orcs rather than Goblins. Grom was to prove the exception, a Goblin whose size rivalled the greatest Orc Warbosses of the time, and whose drive to conquer outweighed them all. Grom was not especially tall (certainly not as tall as an Orc) but he was enormously strong and infamously fat. In fact he was so huge that he became known as The Paunch of Misty Mountain, or simply Grom the Fat.

THE BATTLE OF IRON GATE

For a number of years Grom's Broken Axe tribe wandered the southern Worlds Edge Mountains and the Badlands, conquering the Orcs and Goblins that dwelt there. Some time around the year 2410 Grom led his horde through Black Fire Pass and then northwards along the Dwarf-held highlands. In a matter of weeks, he brought several small Dwarf holds to ruin, desecrated the tombs of Dwarf ancestors and ordered an ancient and colossal statue of the Dwarf god Grungni hacked into his own, not insubstantial, image. Furious at Grom's atrocities, the Dwarfs cursed his name and gathered their forces to hew his flesh.

At the Battle of Iron Gate, the army of King Bragarik faced Grom's horde. After a long and hard-fought battle, the two sides retreated leaving many dead on the field but no clear victor. For the Dwarfs it was a disaster. Grom's rusty axe had reaped a grim tally of many of the King's best warriors and all hope of driving the horde away were gone. In desperation, the Dwarfs sent emissaries to the Empire to seek help.

THE FALL OF NULN

Unfortunately for the Dwarfs (and for the Empire) the reigning Emperor was Dieter IV, the Elector Count of Stirland, perhaps the most feckless and callow individual ever to sit upon the Imperial throne. When the Dwarf King's messenger reached Dieter's Golden Palace in Nuln, the Emperor reacted immediately, not by sending help, but by removing his entire court westwards to Altdorf in order to be as far as possible from the threat of Grom's horde. Disgusted, the Dwarf messenger returned to Karaz-a-Karak where the King received the news of the Emperor's decision with stoicism and a fresh entry in the Book of Grudges. Unable to contain the Goblin Warlord's ambitions without aid, the Dwarfs resolved to shut their stout doors and defend their holds from within.

As the Waaagh! rampaged uncontested over the Worlds Edge Mountains it was joined by the Night Goblin tribes of Red Eye Mountain and many Forest Goblin tribes. With his armies growing in numbers and strength, Grom drove further and further west, devastating much of Stirland, Talabecland and even penetrating as far as Hochland in the shadow of the Middle Mountains. Empire armies were met and defeated with snaggle-toothed glee, and much of the countryside was abandoned. Nuln, whose city defences had long been neglected in favour of marbled magnificence, was attacked and overrun in short order. For several days, the cobblestone streets of Nuln rang to the sound of reckless chariot racing. Dieter's Golden Palace was stripped of its finery to be put into service as a squig pen.

THE SACK OF AN EMPIRE

Grom's horde moved westward until the whole Empire became a land under siege. Communities driven from the countryside huddled behind the heavily defended walls of the cities while outside the greenskins roamed, plundered, maimed and bickered at will. Averheim's walls were held only through the combined efforts of the city militia and no less than five knightly orders. The fortified city of Middenheim became a virtual island amongst a seething sea of green bodies. The Moot was awash with Goblins who, in the Halflings, had finally found something they could torment with impunity. The Emperor did nothing but skulk behind the walls of Altdorf and dream of better days, lissome maidens and rivers of gold. Only the desperate valour of Prince Wilhelm, cousin to Dieter, and his citizen army held Altdorf secure from the greenskins.

Whilst Prince Wilhelm preserved the Reikland, Grom shifted the focus of his rampage northwards. At Middenheim, Grom himself led a charge through the breached gate, pausing only to bellow at his

subordinates for their inability 'ter take a town from der squishies'. Bored and thoroughly disgusted with the lack of fight to be had in this part of the Empire, Grom gave thought to the next stage of his campaign. His mind made up, Grom set off for the coast, pausing only to build a magnificent (and, by necessity, sturdy) chariot from the roof timbers of a temple of the White Wolf. Such was Grom's haste, Middenheim was left relatively intact, save for the roofless temple, a decidedly ruined gate and a lingering smell. With a new goal fixed firmly in his tiny mind, Grom reached the shores of the ocean in short order.

THE HORDE PASSES WEST

Upon reaching the coast, Grom ordered the construction of a huge fleet of ships. Acres of forest were felled to provide the timber, and whole tribes of Goblins were sent to forage for materials amongst the ruins of the Empire. For weeks the makeshift forges bellowed and Goblins sweated as the ramshackle armada took shape. It was a fleet whose like had never been seen before; vast hulks of crudely fashioned wood propelled by massive treadwheels, gigantic ragged sails and feverishly straining Snotlings.

When Grom set sail and made his way along the coast, he was shadowed by a fleet of ships from the Empire. Admiral von Kronitze did not want to risk engaging the Goblin armada if at all possible, reckoning that time, tide and greenskin naval ineptitude would do much of the work for him. Alas, as the fleets approached Marienburg, freak weather drove them into a bloody battle that saw half the Imperial ships sent to the bottom of the sea and the rest scattered to the four winds. The Goblins themselves lost dozens of vessels to the storm, each crammed to the gunnels with panicked greenskins. With his fleet battered, Grom intended to seek fresh timber upon the Marienburg shorelands, but as evening fell the weather grew wilder still. Though Grom ranted and railed at his crew, the gusting winds easily overcame the efforts of toiling greenskins and the gargantuan Goblin's fleet was blown westwards once more.

After forty nights at sea, Grom's fleet made landfall on Ulthuan. Disembarking from the ships, the Goblin hordes ravaged the Elven realm as they had done the lands of the Old World, roasting captured Elves by the score and pounding the elegant Elven cities to rubble. Grom's Waaagh! was finally spent before the walls of Tor Yvresse, but not before his head Shaman accidentally disrupted a waystone, nearly unleashing an unstoppable magic vortex that could have doomed the world. No one is entirely sure what happened to Grom in the wake of that conflict. Regardless of his ultimate fate, Grom's name remains loathed and feared in all corners of the world, save for a few dark corners of the Badlands where skulking Goblins believe his corpulent majesty will return and lead them to victory once again.

WAAAGH! SKARSNIK

Chieftain of arguably the most powerful Night Goblin tribe in the known world, Skarsnik of the Crooked Moons is an outstandingly devious and sneaky individual in a race that exemplifies such traits. In traditional Goblin fashion, Skarsnik's meteoric ascension was supported by the untimely (yet wholly explicable) deaths of a long succession of chief rivals. As such, when Warboss Ibrit Dungstrangler had an improbable yet terminal encounter with a jug of lamp oil, a nest of cave hornets and Skarsnik's pet squig, Gobbla, Skarsnik seized control of the tribe.

From the day that Skarsnik wrested leadership, the fortunes of the Crooked Moon tribe increased markedly. In a series of carefully crafted betrayals, Skarsnik subjugated the other greenskin tribes who had taken up residence in the upper halls of Karak Eight Peaks, an ancient Dwarfen realm now contested by Goblins, Dwarfs and Skaven. Skarsnik then turned his gaze to the Skaven-infested tunnels below, paying a tribute of 'docile' squigs to the Warlord of Clan Mors (in reality, the beasts had been induced into a stupor by a carefully brewed fungus potion). A week later, after the passages no longer rang to the sound of snapping teeth and panicked ratmen, Skarsnik led an army to claim much of the now notably empty (and bloodstained) caverns in the process.

It was about this time that a Dwarf throng under the leadership of Duregar approached Skarsnik's domain, with the aim of reinforcing the army of Belegar, king of the surviving Dwarf citadel in Karak Eight Peaks. Occupied though he was with maintaining control over his tribe and his new territories, Skarsnik had spite enough to spare for this new rival and directed an army of greenskins to assail the Dwarfs as they advanced into Mad Dog Pass.

As Duregar's force entered the mouth of the pass, they were beset from the rear by Orcs whilst countless Goblins emerged from caves and poured down the slope. Confronted with such large numbers of bloodthirsty greenskins, the Dwarfs were hard-pressed and only their stubborn tenacity allowed them to endure long enough for their cannons to turn the course of the battle. The Dwarfs celebrated their victory, unaware that the many hundreds of greenskins that had been slain in Mad Dog Pass amounted to but a fraction of Skarsnik's true strength (and coincidentally all hailed from a clan that Skarsnik had a certain antipathy towards). Meanwhile, having tested Duregar's resolve, Skarsnik prepared his true attack.

So it was that the Dwarfs again found themselves assailed, this time at the East Gate of Death Pass. As Duregar marched towards the lofty mountain gate he found his army surrounded by a horde of cackling greenskins and the gate's grim watchtower held against him. Outnumbered and trapped, the dismayed Dwarfs resolved to sell their lives dearly. And so they did. Only the last-minute intervention of King Belegar, whose forces struck from Karak Eight Peaks, saw the scant survivors of Duregar's force through to the safety of the gate. As a sickly moon cast its light upon Death Pass, Skarsnik was the master of the battlefield.

The Battle of East Gate was a disaster for the Dwarfs – more than half their number lay dead on the skree-covered slopes and, though Skarsnik's losses were more numerous, his horde could well afford to lose as many again. Content with his victory, and uninterested in attacking the Dwarfs head on, Skarsnik now waits until they venture outside their citadel at Karak Eight Peaks and then picks them off one by one, capturing the stragglers alive if possible, and tormenting them for days within earshot of the citadel walls.

It is in this way that Skarsnik has amassed a steadily growing collection of Dwarf beards. Displayed on long wooden stakes, they twitch in the chill mountain breezes and serve as a warning to any that seek to challenge the Warlord of the Eight Peaks. Skarsnik's fame has grown amongst the other tribes, and all greenskins for leagues around Karak Eight Peaks hail him as their undisputed master.

WAAAGH! AZHAG

Azhag the Slaughterer was never the same after he won the Crown of Sorcery in the ruins of Todtheim, for the Liche Nagash's insidious spirit still clung to the circlet and began to dominate the Orc's uncomplicated psyche. From that day forth, Azhag's primal power was combined with the tactical genius and arcane fury of the ancient Liche.

Though he was never truly able to convince his followers as to the value of turning an enemy's flank, the new-found insights Azhag gained from the crown allowed him to make short work of the rival Warbosses who stood in his path. Prior to each battle, Azhag would dictate the plan of attack, speaking in a decidedly un-Orcy voice that seemed heavy with the weight of centuries, and then bellow at his ladz to get moving. Such successes swiftly gained him a huge following of greenskins – they didn't care that Azhag spoke funny, just as long as he 'showed 'em where da fighting wuz.'

As his horde marched into the Empire, Azhag's strategies became ever more complex. This led to, amongst other things, the infamous synchronised Goblin attack waves at the Battle of Dark Moor and the dastardly Snotling pincer assaults at Butcher's Hill. Those foes that exemplary tactics did not vanquish were easily dispatched by the dark magics that the crown placed at Azhag's command. With brain and brawn so closely aligned, it seemed that no force could stop Azhag's Waaagh!

Azhag finally met his match at the Battle of Osterwald. Werner von Kreigstadt, the Grand Master of the Knights Panther, slew Azhag and left the Waaagh! leaderless. After the battle, the Orc horde dispersed into the forests and hills. As for the Crown of Sorcery, it was recovered by the Grand Theogonist who took it back to Altdorf and placed it in the deepest vault of the Temple of Sigmar to be guarded for eternity by powerful spells.

WAAAGH! GRIMGOR

No one knows the early history of Grimgor Ironhide. All that is known is that he staggered out of the Blasted Wastes with a grizzled, bloody and much-scarred bodyguard. Grimgor easily took over the first tribe he met, conquered the second and annihilated the third.

Even for an Orc, Grimgor's thirst for battle is exceptional. If a single day passes without sight of a foe he starts bloody-minded arguments, his one good eye leering out from a mass of scars to find fault with those around him. Two days of relative peace and Grimgor kills any Goblins unfortunate enough to come within arm's reach. Should three days pass without violent release, Grimgor's army is in trouble.

Within a month of his arrival in the Worlds Edge Mountains, Grimgor had hacked himself a sizeable realm. Before a year had passed he had brought Karak Kadrin under siege, baking countless captives in their armour until the ramshackle Orc camp reeked of smouldering Dwarf. As winter came on, Ironhide led his horde down the mountains and into Kislev, carving the countryside to ruin before freezing cold and driving blizzards cast him back.

In the wake of his invasion of Kislev, Grimgor decided to find a base from which to strike, swiftly and bloodily seizing control of Karak Ungor from the Red Eye Goblins. For many years thereafter, Grimgor would lead his followers into Kislev during the spring, retreating to his stronghold in the winter months and sating his bloodlust against the seemingly never-ending supply of Skaven nestled in the mountain's depths. In recent years, however, Grimgor has grown weary of this and now seeks a foe that can truly challenge his might. In the ensuing blood-soaked Waaagh!, Elven Lords and Dwarf Kings have fallen to Grimgor's axe by the dozen and scores of villages and towns have been laid waste. Even Archaon, the Everchosen of Chaos, has been humbled before Ironhide, whose growing concern is that he will never find a battle worthy of his murderous talents.

IMPORTANT EVENTS

The story of the Orcs and Goblins is told in the countless Waaaghs! launched against other lands. These battles are, in keeping with the nature of the greenskins, timeless – the names of warlords and tribes may change, but the bloodthirsty character of the race is evident through the ages.

Imperial Calendar

-1500　The Elves abandon the Old World and the declining Dwarf empire is destroyed by earthquakes and volcanic eruptions. Orcs and Goblins pour over the lands, looting and destroying the remaining Elf cities and destroying Dwarf holds. The Dwarfs refer to the next five hundred years as the time of the Goblin Wars as the Dwarfs and Goblins fight for control of the old Dwarf empire. The first hold to fall is that of Karak Ungor, thereafter known as Red Eye Mountain.

-1498　Orc Warlord Argor Foespike captures the Dwarf mine at Ekrund, renaming it Mount Bloodhorn and turning its resources to the fabrication of the heaviest armour his Boyz can bear.

-1457　The rich Dwarf mines of Mount Gunbad fall to the Bloody Spear Night Goblins, who hold it against ongoing attack from the jealous Red Face Goblins inhabiting the surrounding mountains.

-1387　The Silver Road Wars begin between the Dwarfs and the Goblins. At their height, only one Dwarfen caravan in five survives the journey through the greenskin-infested Deadrock Gap.

-1367　The Orc Warlord Urk Grimfang seizes control of Mount Silverspear from the Dwarfs. It is thereafter known as Mount Grimfang.

-1245　Dwarfs drive the Orcs from the mountains and gain control of the whole area between Karak Kadrin and Mad Dog Pass. Mount Gunbad is temporarily recaptured by the Dwarfs but then lost again. Mount Grimfang is attacked but the Dwarfs are beaten off by Orc Chieftain Nurk Ard'ed.

c.-1200　Nagash the Black excavates the Cursed Pit. Goblins and Orcs flee west to escape the necromantic evil that grips the south.

-975　Battle of a Thousand Woes. A Dwarf attempt to recapture Red Eye Mountain is thwarted when their army is ambushed north of Karak Kadrin. The Dwarfs give up their attempted reconquests.

-750　The Red Cloud Goblins discover a long-lost Dwarfen passage linking the Red Cloud and Fire Mountains. They use this secret way to attack and partially occupy the hold of Karak Azul.

-740　Bitter infighting in the ranks of the Red Cloud Goblins allows the Dwarfs to reclaim control of Karak Azul, though the passage beneath the mountains must be guarded for all time lest the Goblins infiltrate through it once more.

c.-513　After long resistance, the Dwarf hold of Karak Eight Peaks succumbs to repeated attacks from greenskins and Skaven. The victors thereafter battle each other for control of the depths.

-469　Orc Warlord Dork leads a huge army of greenskins to take the Dwarf hold of Karak Azgal which he destroys and abandons, leaving the depths unexplored.

-466　Karak Drazh is occupied by Dork's forces and renamed Black Crag. All the mountains between Mad Dog Pass and Karak Eight Peaks are in Orc and Goblin hands.

-370　The rampages of Urgok the Beard Burner. Orcs and Goblins almost overwhelm the remaining Dwarf holds but are finally beaten back at the Battle of Black Water.

-15-50　The time of Sigmar. Orcs and Goblins are driven out of the lands west of the Worlds Edge Mountains. A massive Orc army is defeated at the Battle of Black Fire Pass (Imperial Year -1).

977　Gilles the Breton conquers all the lands west of the Grey Mountains and creates the realm of Bretonnia. Many Orcs and Goblins retreat to the Grey Mountains and northern forests, and are eventually repulsed entirely from the land.

c.1705　Around this time Gorbad Ironclaw defeats Crusher Zogoth and unites the Ironclaw and Broken Tooth tribes at the fortress of Iron Rock.

1707 - 1712　The greatest Orc Warlord of all time, Gorbad Ironclaw, leads a huge Waaagh! into the Empire, sacking Averheim and Nuln and destroying the state of Solland. Altdorf is beseiged and Emperor Sigismund is slain.

2201　King Louen Orc Slayer of Bretonnia begins the Errantry Wars by declaring his intention to rid his realm of Orcs. Over the next century, Bretonnian territory is gradually cleared of greenskins, who take to the mountains and forests to escape the king's knights.

2302　The Great War. Some greenskins fight alongside the forces of Chaos, others attack warbands as they pass into the Empire, giving rise to rumours of vile, mutated Chaos Goblins.

2420　Bretonnian King Charlen annouces his intention to carry the Errantry Wars east into the Border Princes and beyond. Bretonnian Knights win a huge victory against the Orcs at Blood River.

2420 - 2424　Grom the Paunch of Misty Mountain leads a coalition of unwilling Orc and Goblins tribes into the Worlds Edge Mountains. After defeating the Dwarfs at the Battle of Iron Gate, the Waaagh! moves into the Empire, burning Nuln to the ground. Grom leads his army to the sea where he builds a huge fleet and sails into the west, landing on the shores of Ulthuan. His rampage continues in the Elf realm until he is finally defeated by an Elven host led by Eltharion the Grim.

2470 The Goblin warlord Boggrub Legbiter leads the Broken Nose tribe against the Dwarfs of Karak-Azul, capturing from them two mighty war machines, which they dub the Skull Crusher and the Lead Belcher. Armed with these terrible machineries of destruction, Boggrub carves a path of destruction through the Worlds Edge Mountains and into Averland.

2488 The Battle of Death Pass. A Bretonnian army is defeated by Morglum Necksnapper. The Bretonnian king declares the Errantry Wars at an end.

2498 The Battle of the Jaws. In the depths of Mad Dog Pass, Skarsnik vanquishes a Dwarf army in a cunning ambush.

2500 - 2510 Orc Warlord Gnashrak unites the Orcs and Goblins of the eastern Worlds Edge Mountains and leads a huge army along the Silver Road towards Karaz a Karak. The Orcs rampage through the mountains for years, threatening to capture the capital. Eventually Gnashrak is defeated at the Battle of Broken Leg Gulley by a Dwarf army led by Ungrim Ironfist of Karak Kadrin.

2503 - 2507 An Orc army under Gorfang Rotgut besieges Barak Varr and later joins up with Orc and Goblin tribes led by Morglum Necksnapper to attack Karak Azul. The Orcs briefly take possession of parts of the hold and capture many kinsfolk of Lord Kazador.

2510 A Goblin horde led by the infamous Night Goblin Warboss, Spinny Backstab, rampages through the farmsteads surrounding Middenheim, razing to the ground over a hundred farms and villages. Backstab is eventually defeated by the celebrated Middenmarshal Kurt Heinwald, and the timely intervention of a steam tank dispatched in haste from Nuln.

In the same year, the formerly unremarkable Goblin Boss Gorblum Yellowstreak cons an enchanted crown from an Orc Shaman, utilises its formidable powers of command to gather an army, and renames himself Gorblum the Magnificent. He goes on to achieve notoriety as he slaughters a Dwarf throng under King Thorgrim and rampages across half the Worlds Edge Mountains.

2512 - 2515 Given inspiration and counsel by the whispering voice in his head, Azhag the Slaughterer leads a huge army of Orcs and Night Goblins into the northern Empire, burning and pillaging vast swathes of land.

2257 The Storm of Chaos. Grimgor Ironhide bests the Chaos Everchosen, Archaon, in single combat before the gates of Middenheim.

BESTIARY

This section of the book details the forces of a greenskin horde. As well as giving special rules that govern the army as a whole, it also describes how each unit and individual fights, as well as any special rules that apply. In the latter part, we detail the primal fury of Orcy Waaagh! magic and the powerful magical artefacts that greenskins take to battle.

ARMY SPECIAL RULES

ANIMOSITY

When greenskins get together they start to pick fights, bicker and misbehave in all sorts of appalling ways. Even at the best of times, squabbling in the ranks can send a greenskin horde into disarray. One moment a mob is striding purposefully towards the enemy, and the next it is brought to a halt whilst two or more greenies settle their differences.

TESTING FOR ANIMOSITY

At the beginning of the movement phase (before declaring charges) in each of your turns you must test for Animosity. All of your units on the table are subject to Animosity, except:

- Fleeing units.
- Units in close combat.
- Units of fewer than five models.
- War machines and chariots.
- Units of Snotlings, Trolls, Giants and Black Orcs.

Starting on one side of the table and working through your army, roll a D6 for each unit that is subject to Animosity and consult the Animosity table (shown to the right).

CHARACTERS AND ANIMOSITY

Obviously, being single models, characters do not test for Animosity if they are alone. If they have joined a unit, they are bound by that unit's Animosity test and must act accordingly.

THE ANIMOSITY TABLE

D6 Result

1 **Squabble.** *Ratgut is a filthy lyin' git and he spat on my favourite boots. He needs teachin' a lesson.* An internal squabble amongst the ranks soon grows into a minor riot with fists and curses flying. This throws the unit into disorder and it can do nothing this turn (including cast spells) whilst da Boss cracks heads.

2-5 **Plan's a good 'un.** *The rest of da army is just softies compared to us. We'll show 'em how it's done.* The unit retains a degree of order. It may act normally this turn.

6 **We'll show 'em!** *We're gonna stomp 'em to dust! Charge!* Infused by the power of the Waaagh! the unit dashes towards the enemy, cheering, waving weapons and jeering at their foes. The unit immediately moves D6" towards the nearest visible enemy by the shortest route, applying the usual penalties for terrain, turning and wheeling, etc. If no enemy is visible, they instead move directly forwards.

If this move takes the unit into contact with an enemy, it is counted as a charge – the moving unit need not take any Psychology tests that would normally be incurred for such a charge. An enemy unit charged in this way may only choose to hold or flee as a charge reaction.

This extra move is an exception to the normal turn sequence. The unit may still move, charge, shoot, cast spells and fight just as normal, but counts as having moved that turn.

WAAAGH!

A truly inspiring Warboss can often rouse his followers to an unparalleled burst of destructive enthusiasm. Once per game, the Orcs & Goblins player can declare a Waaagh! at the start of his turn, before Animosity rolls are made. This ability may only be used if the general is on the table and is not fleeing.

In the turn that a Waaagh! is called:

• The general automatically counts as having rolled a 6 on the Animosity table, as does his unit (even if they would not usually test).

• All units must add their rank bonus to their Animosity rolls. Units of Goblins receive a maximum bonus of +1 (their squeaky voices don't Waaagh! properly).

• All units that are led by one or more Warbosses or Bigbosses receive a +1 bonus to their Animosity rolls that turn.

• Black Orc regiments and Black Orc characters on their own are counted as having rolled a 6, even though they do not normally test. Black Orc characters in units are bound by their unit's test.

A roll of 1 is always a squabble, regardless of any modifiers. In addition, units that squabble in the turn in which a Waaagh! is called suffer D6 Wounds (distributed as for shooting) with no armour saves allowed.

SIZE MATTERS

As a rule, all breeds of Orcs and Goblins expect the smaller greenskins to run away and it doesn't really alarm them when they do. The sight of fleeing or destroyed little 'uns simply reminds the bigger and bolder members of the horde why they are best – a mentality that has even spread to Trolls and Giants. To represent this:

• Goblins do not take Panic tests caused by Snotlings.

• Orcs (and war machines crewed by an Orc Bully) do not take Panic tests caused by Snotlings, Squigs or Goblins (including chariots and war machines crewed by Snotlings or Goblins).

• Black Orcs do not take Panic tests caused by Snotlings, Squigs, Goblins or Orcs (including chariots and war machines).

• Trolls only take Panic tests caused by other Trolls and Giants.

• Giants only take Panic tests caused by other Giants.

ORCS

Orcs vary a great deal in size and appearance, with the biggest individuals in charge of the rest. Pecking order is established by constant fighting, so only the meanest and nastiest Orcs get to the very top of the tribal ladder. Even the smallest Orc packs a great deal of bone, muscle and bloody-mindedness into a body no taller than a Man's, but which is substantially broader. Orcs have huge jaws, and tiny foreheads behind which lurk a thick skull and not much in the way of brain.

Orcs live in tribes, a collection of greenskins ruled over by the largest, strongest and loudest Boss, an individual known as a Big Boss or a Warboss, depending on his stature. These tribes might only exist as long as the Orc leading them can hold their fractious elements together, or until a challenger usurps power, invariably slaying the old Boss in a leadership challenge, and moulding the tribe to his own, unique vision. There are many tribes, and they are often colourfully named, after their leader, their deeds or some unusual characteristic or custom exhibited by them. Some particularly infamous tribes include the Ironclaw Orcs, the Red Fang Orcs, the Orcs of the Bloody Hand, and the rarely seen White Orcs of Mount Grimfang.

Orcs, and indeed all greenskins, worship their own gods who they call Gork and Mork – the former "fighty but kunnin'", the latter "kunnin' but fighty". Their faith in their gods is made terrifyingly real through the phenomenon of the Waaagh! During the intense excitement of battle the magical field unconsciously focused by all greenskins becomes stronger until the horde is swept up in an explosion of violence so intense that it will only begin to abate when every last enemy (or Orc) is slain.

The power of the Waaagh! serves not only to drive the Orcs and Goblins forward in battle, but also to fuel the magic of their crazed Shamans. The Waaagh! always discharges through the most receptive mind, that of an Orc or Goblin Shaman. In immature Orcs this takes the form of random visions and crackling green energy, but mature Shamans have learned how to control these powers and turn them to their advantage in the form of powerful blasts and awesome spells of destruction.

	M	WS	BS	S	T	W	I	A	Ld
Orc	4	3	3	3	4	1	2	1	7
Orc Big 'Un	4	4	3	4	4	1	2	1	7
Orc Boss	4	4	3	4	4	1	2	2	7
Orc Big Boss	5	5	3	4	5	2	3	3	8
Orc Warboss	4	6	3	5	5	3	4	4	9
Orc Shaman	4	3	3	3	4	2	2	1	7
Great Shaman	4	3	3	4	5	3	2	1	8

WARGEAR

Choppa. Orcish weapons are crude things that rely less on keen edges and more on sheer mass. In the hands of an Orc, such weapons are incredibly deadly, able to bludgeon a foe into a bloody mess in very short order. Such a chunk of metal would be difficult for a human to wield in one hand, but Orcs are muscle-bound beasts with fists as big as a Man's head. Choppas are hand weapons in all respects. They also confer a +1 Strength bonus to models on foot in the first round of each combat.

ORC BOAR BOYZ

Orc Boar Boyz are rough, tough and very determined. War boars are evil-minded creatures that will take every opportunity to maim, bite and kick the enemy and also their Orc masters. Breaking in a war boar can be a long and dangerous business, but Orcs have thick skulls and don't feel much pain. In fact, you never really train a war boar, you just learn to hang on better while the creature goes crazy, goring and stamping, twisting and biting, and generally causing as much damage as it can.

	M	WS	BS	S	T	W	I	A	Ld
Boar Boy	4	3	3	3	4	1	2	1	7
Big 'Un	4	4	3	4	4	1	2	1	7
Boar Boy Boss	4	4	3	4	4	1	2	2	7
Boar	7	3	0	3	4	1	3	1	3

Choppa. See page 18.

SPECIAL RULES

Thick-skinned. A boar rider receives an armour save bonus of +2 rather than the usual +1 for ordinary cavalry mounts.

Tusker Charge. A charging boar is a bad-tempered mound of bloody-minded muscle with pointy tusks and a bad attitude. A boar therefore receives +2 Strength during the turn in which it charges.

Big 'Uns

The largest Orcs in a tribe, and therefore most important, are known as Big 'Uns. These Big 'Uns are even stronger and meaner than other Orcs, and far more formidable on the battlefield.

ORC BOAR CHARIOTS

Orcs use chariots as fast, mobile weapons of war. Not only are they powerful but they also look good! Chariot riders like to ride around at high speed, displaying their obvious superiority over more lowly greenskins. To make the chariots even more obviously important, the Orcs invariably strap the biggest banners they can find (as well as shields, trophies and the heads of slain foes) to every surface of the chariot.

The rest of the army either ignores these show-offs or throws things in their direction, like rocks, insults or the smaller members of their unit.

	M	WS	BS	S	T	W	I	A	Ld
Chariot	–	–	–	5	5	4	–	–	–
Orc	–	3	–	3	–	–	2	1	7
Boar	7	3	–	3	–	–	3	1	–

Choppa. See page 18.

SPECIAL RULES
Chariot; Tusker Charge (see above).

19

BLACK ORCS

Black Orcs are the biggest and strongest of all Orcs, and get their name from their dour, grim demeanour as much as from the colour of their skin, which is extremely dark green or black. They are bigger than normal Orcs and pride themselves on being the best fighters of all. They take war much more seriously than other Orcs and have the best equipment. Many of their fearsome weapons are captured in battle, and carried as a mark of their self-evident superiority, while others are paid in tribute by subjugated tribes.

The origins of the Black Orcs are shrouded in mystery, but some maintain they they were created by the Chaos Dwarfs of the Dark Lands, perhaps to serve as slaves or warriors. Certainly, the Black Orcs' sturdy constitution would allow them to prosper in the harsh land of the Chaos Dwarfs when lesser greenskin workers would perish. They first appeared in the Old World during Sigmar's time, perhaps escaping or being expelled from the lands of their supposed creators, a whole band crossing the Worlds Edge Mountains and conquering the other Orcs living in the hills to the northwest of Stirland. When Sigmar first united the Men of the middle Old World into the Empire, he had first to drive out the Orcs and Goblins that lived there. Those battles

against the Black Orcs were by far the hardest fought, and only won at terrible cost to Sigmar's armies. Black Orcs regard other Orcs and Goblins with contempt, especially Goblins, who are always running away instead of standing and fighting. In battle, Black Orcs keep a constant eye out for bickering in the ranks, and it takes little more than a dark scowl or a throaty growl from a single Black Orc to bring the lesser greenskins into line. Should that fail, Black Orcs are perfectly willing, and exceptionally able, to wade in and smash some heads together, thus restoring order quick smart at the insignificant cost of the lives of the wrongdoers.

	M	WS	BS	S	T	W	I	A	Ld
Black Orc	4	4	3	4	4	1	2	1	8
Black Orc Boss	4	5	3	4	4	1	2	2	8
Black Orc Big Boss	4	6	3	4	5	2	3	3	8
Black Orc Warboss	4	7	3	5	5	3	4	4	9

Choppa. See page 18.

SPECIAL RULES

Quell Animosity. When Animosity strikes a mob of Boyz, Orc Bosses tend to get caught up in the brawl that results. Black Orc Bosses, on the other hand, 'don't stand fer any of dat bovver' and swiftly restore order with extreme prejudice (and a big axe). If a Black Orc character is in a unit that rolls a 'squabble' result in an Animosity test, he immediately inflicts D6 Strength 5 hits on his unit in the process of restoring order. The hits are distributed as for shooting, but may not be allocated to the Black Orc. The unit is then treated as having rolled a 'Plan's a good 'un' result.

Armed to da teef. As a rule, Black Orcs tend to turn up to battle with as many weapons as they can carry. Every Black Orc prides himself on the breadth and depth of his arsenal, from small choppas kept handy for close encounters with little 'uns, to larger, two-handed, armaments for bludgeoning more stubborn foes. At the start of each combat, a unit of Black Orcs can choose to fight either with single choppa (in case they have shields), two choppas or with a great weapon. If a Black Orc character chooses a magic weapon, he loses the benefit of this special rule.

SAVAGE ORCS

Long ago all Orcs lived in the south, and were savages with no means of manufacturing metal weapons, armour or war machines. These primitive Orcs used flint spears, wooden clubs, and whatever other weaponry they could steal from more advanced races. As the tribes expanded, migrating northwards in the earliest of Waaagh!s, they learned the secret of metal working from the Chaos Dwarfs. A few tribes, however, missed out, got hopelessly lost, were left behind in the south or perhaps deliberately turned their back on the new ways.

Savage Orcs persist in their primitive ways to this day. Upon the eve of battle, Savage Orc Shamans daub crude tattoos onto the warriors' bodies. Such is their faith in the power of the Orc gods Gork and Mork to protect them that enemy arrows and sword blows really can be deflected by the aura of self-generated Orcy faith.

Savage Orcs are a complete bunch of primitives, even by Orcish standards. They use mostly stone or bone weapons and go around half-naked, or worse. Many live in their own tribes and have their own ways of fighting that make them easily distinguishable. Others are the oddballs of more 'Orcy' tribes, small groups that have 'gone native' in the belief that the 'old ways is best'. Some Savage Orcs ride to battle upon mighty war boars, one of the few creatures in the world as bad tempered as the Savage Orcs themselves.

Unsurprisingly, Savage Orcs and war boars get on famously well, sharing as they do an almost identical world-view and personal hygiene regimen.

	M	WS	BS	S	T	W	I	A	Ld
Savage Orc	4	3	3	3	4	1	2	1	7
Savage Orc Big 'Un	4	4	3	4	4	1	2	1	7
Savage Orc Boss	4	4	3	4	4	1	2	2	7
Savage Orc Big Boss	4	5	3	4	5	2	3	3	8
Savage Orc Warboss	4	6	3	5	5	3	4	4	9
Savage Orc Shaman	4	3	3	3	4	2	2	1	7
Savage Orc Great Shaman	4	3	3	4	5	3	2	1	8
Boar	7	3	0	3	4	1	3	1	3

Choppa. See page 18.

SPECIAL RULES

Frenzy.

Warpaint. Savage Orcs adorn themselves with warpaint, tattoos and charms in the belief they will attract the favour of Gork (or possibly Mork). Such is a Savage Orc's faith in his warpaint that he gets a 6+ ward save.

Thick-skinned; Tusker Charge (Boar Boyz only, see page 19)

GOBLINS

Goblins are small, vicious, mean-spirited and generally unpleasant creatures. Clues as to their character may be discerned in their tiny pointed teeth, beady glinting eyes, scrawny grasping hands and general demeanour of a whipped dog. They fight amongst themselves both on and off the battlefield. They feel little sense of loyalty to their own kind, let alone anyone else, and will cheerfully maim, kill and even eat their comrades if they think they can get away with it, often just for a laugh. Many Goblins live amongst their larger Orcish cousins, but others live in great nomadic tribes. While a small number rise to become Goblin Bosses, or are born to become Shamans, most live short, miserable lives punctuated by terrifying periods of intense violence, before being eaten or trodden on by an Orc, or skewered upon the blade of an angry foe.

One thing Goblins do have going for them is that they are numerous – there are lots of them and no matter how many die or run away there always seems to be plenty left. Their preferred method of fighting is to shoot the enemy in the back from a good distance, but failing that, a long spear rates a distant second best. Goblins are generally poor and often unwilling fighters, but are dangerous in large groups and quite capable of overwhelming far better troops by sheer weight of numbers.

Many Goblin tribes manifest enormous variety in custom, environment and way of life, such as the spider-riding Forest Goblins that infest the dark woodlands of the Border Princes, or the One-Eyed Goblins of Blind River, whose bizarre self-mutilation is utterly inexplicable to other Goblinoids. There exist many other types of Goblin, some very different from the normal run of greenskin, and the subject of conjecture, myth or outright fairy tale. These include the light-fingered Gnoblars of the Mountains of Mourn, the noisome Bogarts of the Marshes of Madness, and the nocturnal Mere-Goblins of Black Water.

Some tribes of Goblins have few or no Orcs to lead them, and here the rather suspect talents of the Goblin Warbosses come into play. A Goblin that finds himself in charge of a Goblin tribe will quickly manifest an acute 'Gork complex', invariably letting the power go entirely to his head. He will often try to emulate a particular Orc Warboss, lauding it over his subordinates, inflicting petty violence and generally being even more unpleasant than is usual for a Goblin. This is only likely to last until a passing Orc notices the Gobbos have no one to lead them, at which point the Goblin Warboss is likely to be booted back into the ranks of his fellows, where he will receive a good thumping for his behaviour.

	M	WS	BS	S	T	W	I	A	Ld
Goblins	4	2	3	3	3	1	2	1	6
Goblin Boss	4	2	3	3	3	1	2	2	6
Goblin Big Boss	4	4	3	4	4	2	3	3	7
Goblin Warboss	4	5	3	4	4	3	4	4	8
Goblin Shaman	4	2	3	3	3	2	2	1	6
Goblin Great Shaman	4	2	3	3	4	3	2	1	7

SPECIAL RULES

Fear Elves. All Goblins dislike fighting Elves of any kind because they 'stink funny' and because their haughty manner unnerves the little greenskins. Goblins therefore Fear any unit of Elves whose unit strength they do not outnumber by at least two to one. Count any Orcs, Squigs or anything else in the unit as well as the Gobbos.

GOBLIN WOLF RIDERS

Many Goblin tribes are nomadic in nature, traversing the wilderness of the Badlands and the steppes to the east in huge, ramshackle caravans, raiding, stealing from, or, at a push, trading with, other greenskins they meet along the way. Roaming Wolf Riders – Goblins mounted upon the backs of swift, snarling giant wolves – precede these snaking trains of scummy Goblinhood. Packs of Wolf Riders scout out the land ahead and pounce upon any foe foolish enough to be caught alone in the wide-open spaces.

Wolf Riders perform a similar task in battle, using their speed and agility to harry the flanks of enemy units and chasing down those already beaten and fleeing the battlefield. Being Goblins, Wolf Riders like to pick on the weak, the isolated, and those already bleeding to death, and their preferred victims are the likes of enemy war machine crew, small units of scouts and those few beings smaller and weaker than themselves.

	M	WS	BS	S	T	W	I	A	Ld
Wolf Rider	4	2	3	3	3	1	2	1	6
Wolf Rider Boss	4	2	3	3	3	1	2	2	6
Giant Wolf	9	3	0	3	3	1	3	1	3

SPECIAL RULES
Fast Cavalry; Fear Elves (see page 22)

GOBLIN WOLF CHARIOTS

Goblin Wolf Chariots are a blatant attempt by the more diminutive greenskins to imitate the boar chariots ridden to war by Orcs. Although Goblins have little trouble getting a saddle on a wolf, the beasts are far less happy to be tethered to a rickety chariot, and many Goblins come to a premature end whilst trying to do so. Nonetheless, once an especially brave or skilful Goblin has, somehow, overcome this obstacle and convinced the wolves to cooperate, he will be the envy of his mates. The rest of the tribe will cheer and applaud as he dashes around the battlefield, cackling uproariously as his chariot careens into the enemy lines, smashing the foe, and sometimes even the driver and the chariot, to smithereens in the process.

	M	WS	BS	S	T	W	I	A	Ld
Chariot	–	–	–	5	4	3	–	–	–
Goblin	–	2	3	3	–	–	2	1	6
Giant Wolf	9	3	–	3	–	–	3	1	–

SPECIAL RULES
Chariot; Fear Elves (see page 22)

NIGHT GOBLINS

Many years ago a tribe of Goblins took to living in the caves beneath the Worlds Edge Mountains. Over the centuries these became distinct in type and are now known as Night Goblins. Night Goblins have become so accustomed to the dark that when they come out into the open they prefer to move around at night and hide away during the day. Many of them wear long ragged cloaks, dangling caps and hooded coats that protect them from the hated sunlight.

Night Goblins raise special subterranean fungi deep beneath the mountains in their cool damp caves. They cultivate many types of fungus and are always searching for new ones to experiment with. Some fungi are used as food for the Night Goblins and the strange animals they breed, but many types are grown for their hallucinogenic or intoxicating properties or because they affect the Goblin metabolism in some other way. These fungi are traded with other Goblins for weapons and many other items the Night Goblins need. Night Goblin Shamans are expert at identifying, growing and using fungi, and they grow many special strains to use as poisons.

Night Goblins often take over abandoned strongholds, and much of the ancient Dwarf empire is now infested with these vile creatures. Occasionally the Dwarfs will try to drive the Goblins out, or the Goblins will find some passage that leads them into Dwarf tunnels, and the two races battle it out beneath the mountains. Due to this ancient enmity Dwarfs and Night Goblins are implacable foes and will often fight to the death rather than give an inch of ground to their foe.

In common with all Goblins, Night Goblins are petty, if cowardly creatures. Where they differ, however, is that their Shamans prepare them for battle by brewing huge quantities of fungus beer, lending them sharper instincts and quicker reactions, if rendering them paranoid and twitchy at the same time. As they get steadily more drunk, they sing loudly so that their voices fill the tunnels of the Worlds Edge Mountains and echo through the Dwarf strongholds. Finally, the dark mountains disgorge the tribe onto the surface, a terrible-smelling wave of cackling, black-hooded death descending upon any foolish or unfortunate enough to stand before it.

	M	WS	BS	S	T	W	I	A	Ld
Night Goblins	4	2	3	3	3	1	3	1	5
Night Goblin Boss	4	2	3	3	3	1	3	2	5
Night Goblin Big Boss	4	4	3	4	4	2	4	3	6
Night Goblin Warboss	4	5	3	4	4	3	5	4	7
Night Goblin Shaman	4	2	3	3	3	2	3	1	5
Night Goblin Great Shaman	4	2	3	3	4	3	3	1	6

SPECIAL RULES

Hate Dwarfs; Fear Elves (see page 22)

Netters. A unit of Night Goblins may be upgraded to carry the capacious nets they use when hunting Cave Squigs – this can be represented by having a handful of Netter models in the unit. At the start of each close combat phase, a unit that contains nets must attempt to entangle one of the units they are fighting. Roll a D6. On a roll of 2-6, the enemy unit has become entangled and suffers a -1 penalty to their Strength until the end of the combat phase. If a 1 is rolled, the Netters have instead managed to cast the nets amongst their own ranks – the Night Goblin unit suffers a -1 penalty to their Strength until the end of the combat phase.

NIGHT GOBLIN FANATICS

A Fanatic is a Night Goblin bearing a ball and chain weapon so large that it would be impossible for a Goblin to pick it up in normal circumstances. Having imbibed a brew made of a very rare and very special fungus called the Mad Cap, the Fanatic's strength is boosted beyond belief, enabling him to swing the heavy ball round and round (and round and round...) in a whirlwind of bone-shattering death.

The Night Goblin is almost completely unaware of what is happening around him, and he has to be carried into battle by his mates. The Night Goblins wait until the enemy are close by, and then push the Fanatic out towards the foe, giving him a good shove to start him off in the right direction. Free at last, the deranged Night Goblin starts to spin round crazily, swinging his ball and chain in a dizzy circle of death. The Fanatic really has little idea of where he is going, and will happily plough through troops from his own side if they get in the way.

	M	WS	BS	S	T	W	I	A	Ld
Fanatic	2D6	–	–	5	3	1	3	D6	10

SPECIAL RULES

Immune to Psychology.

Hide in Night Goblin Units. Fanatics are not placed on the table at the start of the game as are other troops. Instead you must make a written note of any Night Goblin units that include Fanatics. These are referred to as concealing units. Fanatics remain hidden inside concealing units, carried along by their fellows, until they are ready to be pushed out towards the enemy. If a concealing unit flees, any Fanatics yet to be released are lost as they are trampled in the panic.

Force of Destruction. Goblin Fanatics cannot be charged. They may, however, be targeted with missile fire (following the usual -1 penalty for shooting models with a unit strength of 1) or spells.

Release the Fanatics! Fanatics are always released when the concealing unit comes to within 8" of the enemy or vice versa. The moving unit stops immediately (fliers land). Once Fanatic movement has been resolved, the unit can continue moving if the controlling player wishes, although chargers must complete their charge unless panicked (the laws of momentum are particularly harsh). Fanatics can be released in any direction, from any point on the concealing unit and move 2D6". They do not have to be aimed in the direction of the enemy that activated them. If ever a Fanatic's move would end in the middle of a unit, then he automatically bounces through it – place the Fanatic model 1" beyond the unit, in the direction he was moving.

Further Movement. In the turns after they have been released, Fanatics move in the compulsory movement part of the controlling player's movement phase, moving 2D6" in a random direction (determined by the scatter dice).

Splat! When a Fanatic moves through a unit (friend or foe) it immediately inflicts D6 Strength 5 armour piercing hits (for a total of a -3 armour save modifier) on that unit, distributed as for shooting. Units may move and flee through Fanatics, but any foolhardy enough to do so will take hits as described above. A unit that suffers 25% casualties from Fanatics must immediately take a Panic test. Units failing this test flee directly towards the closest table edge (potentially moving through the same Fanatic that triggered the test, suffering a further set of hits).

Out of Control. The life of a Goblin Fanatic is fraught with mishap in the way only the life of a small Goblin orbiting a large metal ball can be. A Fanatic is immediately removed as a casualty when:

• it comes into contact with a terrain feature of any kind.

• it rolls a double for movement – this does not apply in the turn he is released.

• any unit finishes its move over the Fanatic. The unit takes D6 Strength 5 hits for moving into the Fanatic, and a further D6 Strength 5 hits in the Fanatic's death throes.

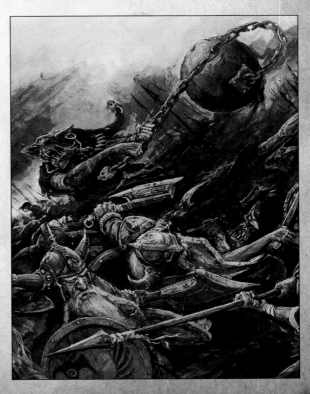

NIGHT GOBLIN SQUIG HERDS

One of the most deadly of all creatures to be found in the deepest caverns is the Cave Squig. These are improbable, hybrid creatures, part fungus and part flesh, with tough, ball shaped bodies, clumsy taloned feet and huge gaping maws.

Night Goblins hunt Cave Squigs using long, sturdy forks called 'prodders' to goad the Squigs from their hiding places and to keep the enraged beasts at bay. In battle, the herders prod and goad their charges into a state of frenzy, before pointing them in the general direction of the enemy.

Squig Herds. Squigs don't fight on their own – they have to be herded into battle by Night Goblins. Night Goblins can be placed anywhere within the unit. Missile hits and impact hits against the unit are randomised as follows: 1-4 hits a Squig, 5-6 hits a Night Goblin Herder. Characters may not join Squig herds.

Wild Squigs. If the unit flees, or if at the start of the controlling player's turn there are no herders alive in the unit, the Squigs go wild. All units within 2D6" (friendly and enemy) immediately take D6 Strength 5 hits to represent the Squigs running amok. After damage is resolved, the unit is removed as a casualty.

	M	WS	BS	S	T	W	I	A	Ld
Night Goblin	4	2	3	3	3	1	3	1	5
Squig	4	4	0	5	3	1	3	2	3

SPECIAL RULES
Hate Dwarfs; Immune to Psychology

NIGHT GOBLIN SQUIG HOPPERS

The most reckless Squig hunters ride Squigs into battle, grabbing hold of the Squig's tiny horns or ears, and bouncing along as the Squig leaps about. These are called Squig Hoppers. It takes a skilled Night Goblin to drive the Squig Hoppers into a coherent mob, because individual Squigs are wont to move in an unpredictable manner while the riders hang on the best they can. Such a Night Goblin can direct his Squig towards the enemy, though he has next to no control of its speed or how far it will leap. Most ferocious of all such creatures are the semi-mythical Great Cave Squigs. If such a beast can be mastered and controlled it can be pressed into service as a most effective (and voracious) battle mount.

	M	WS	BS	S	T	W	I	A	Ld
Squig Hopper	3D6	4	0	5	3	1	3	2	5
Great Cave Squig	3D6	4	0	5	4	3	3	3	3

SPECIAL RULES
May not join units (Great Cave Squig only)

Immune to Psychology; Skirmish; Hate Dwarfs

Boiiing! Squig Hoppers are moved during the compulsory part of the player's movement phase and always travel a full 3D6" in a straight line – the player declares the direction of movement before rolling. If the dice result will bring the Squig Hoppers into contact with an enemy unit, then it is treated as declaring a charge and follows all of the normal rules (eg: the target unit can make a charge response as normal).

DOOM DIVER CATAPULTS

Though the Doom Diver Catapult was first developed as a means of scouting out enemy positions, it didn't take long for some bright spark to try it out in a battle. In the dirty, brutal and often painfully short life of a Goblin, the chance to swoop through the air, cackling madly as he looks down at his former Orcish masters, is often considered just too good to miss. So impressive is the damage and the mess caused by such a plummeting Goblin, that this form of warfare is now taken quite seriously and garners a ridiculous number

of volunteers. It doesn't seem to matter that their chances of survival are negligible, but then only the more crazed or deeply stupid Goblins would want to be propelled high into the air anyway.

	M	WS	BS	S	T	W	I	A	Ld
Catapult	-	-	-	-	7	3	-	-	-
Goblin	4	2	3	3	3	1	2	1	6

SPECIAL RULES

Fear Elves (see page 22)

Doom Diver Catapult. When firing a Doom Diver Catapult treat it as you would a stone thrower (guess range etc.). No template is used with the Doom Diver – if the Goblin hits an enemy model then it automatically causes D6 Strength 5 hits on the unit with no armour saves allowed.

As Doom Divers are able to direct themselves onto their target to some extent, the player is allowed to roll a D3 and move the impact position (after scatter) by this many inches in any direction.

If a Doom Diver should misfire then roll a D6 and consult the stone thrower misfire chart.

ROCK LOBBERS AND SPEAR CHUKKAS

Greenskins make all kinds of contraptions from crude wagons to clanking mills and sturdy war engines. Wood, iron and bone are cheerfully lashed together as required. If things fall apart they can quickly be stuck back together again with spit and string. Goblins are generally more nimble-fingered when it comes to this kind of work whereas Orcs, being bigger, are good at bossing them about. Thus, nature has created the ideal workforce in the greenskin race.

	M	WS	BS	S	T	W	I	A	Ld
Rock Lobber	-	-	-	-	7	3	-	-	-
Spear Chukka	-	-	-	-	7	3	-	-	-
Goblin	4	2	3	3	3	1	2	1	6
Orc Bully	4	3	3	3	4	1	2	1	7

Choppa. (Orc Bully only) See page 18.

SPECIAL RULES

Rock Lobbers. Rock Lobbers are stone throwers.

Spear Chukkas. Spear Chukkas are bolt throwers.

Fear Elves (see page 22)

Stone throwing machines and bolt throwers are common devices in Orc and Goblin armies. Both kinds of machine are usually powered by twisted Squig hide ropes, creating the power required to hurl projectiles across the battlefield. Stone throwers sometimes use a counterweight mechanism to propel their missile. Regardless of their design, greenskins refer to all stone throwers as 'Rock Lobbers' and all bolt throwers as 'Spear Chukkas'.

Orc Bullies

These irascible, infirm and often incontinent old warriors serve an indispensable purpose – ensuring the Goblins crewing the war machines shoot in the right direction and don't run away. Woe betide the Goblin that skives off the day of the big battle!

SNOTLINGS

Snotlings are the smallest of the green-skinned races. They can fetch and carry for other Goblin or Orc races, and perform other odd jobs, so long as these can be explained in single syllable instructions, but they are of little use for any real work. They live around Orcs and Goblins, infesting their caves and huts, scavenging amongst their rubbish piles, and stealing anything they can get their hands on. Larger greenskins regard Snotlings with a certain amount of affection and treat them as wayward and mischievous pets.

When Orcs or Goblins march off to battle they invariably find themselves accompanied by a horde of Snotlings armed with bits of wood, broken spears, and weapons they have stolen or scrounged. When their big friends get stuck into close combat the Snotlings throw themselves on the enemy with a detemination belied by their size, screaming and yelling crazily,

waving their wooden clubs and biting the foes with their sharp teeth. The sheer mass of Snotlings can tie down an enemy unit even if the tiny creatures don't cause many casualties!

	M	WS	BS	S	T	W	I	A	Ld
Snotling base	4	2	0	2	2	3	3	4	

SPECIAL RULES
Immune to Psychology; Stubborn

SNOTLING PUMP WAGON

A Pump Wagon consists of a wooden fighting platform, sometimes taking the form of a ramshackle wooden hut on wheels. It moves under its own power provided, not by horses, wolves or some other beast, but by the frantic pumping of straining Snotlings. This drives a simple mechanism that keeps the Pump Wagon moving, crushing and piercing any foes (and Snotling crew) unfortunate enough to fall beneath it.

	M	WS	BS	S	T	W	I	A	Ld
Pump Wagon	2D6	–	–	4	4	3	–	–	–
Snotling Crew	–	2	–	2	–	–	3	3	4

SPECIAL RULES
Immune to Psychology; Stubborn; Chariot

Oi! Pedal Faster! The Pump Wagon is moved during the compulsory moves part of the player's movement phase. It **always** moves, pursues and flees a full 2D6". The player has no control over the distance moved, but he can decide in which direction to move the Pump Wagon before he rolls the dice. If the dice result will bring the Pump Wagon into contact with an enemy unit, then it is treated as declaring a charge and follows all of the normal rules (eg. the target unit can make a charge response as normal).

Crunch! On the turn a Pump Wagon charges into combat it inflicts 2D6 impact hits.

FOREST GOBLIN SPIDER RIDERS

Forest Goblin tribes are to be found in the depths of many wooded areas, but most are concentrated in a wide forested belt south of the Empire, stretching the length of the Border Princes from Black Fire Pass in the east to Tilea in the west. These forests are full of all kinds of spiders, and the largest of these are sometimes captured and ridden. Spiders are good fighters, with mandibles like steel pincers. They are not as fast as wolves or horses, but spiders can move swiftly over obstacles or rough territory thanks to their many legs.

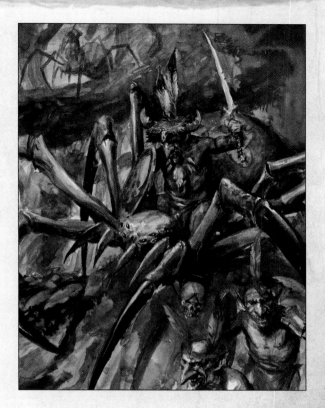

	M	WS	BS	S	T	W	I	A	Ld
Spider Rider	4	2	3	3	3	1	2	1	6
Spider Rider Boss	4	2	3	3	3	1	2	2	6
Giant Spider	7	3	0	3	3	1	4	1	2
Gigantic Spider	7	3	0	4	4	3	4	3	7

SPECIAL RULES

Wall-crawlers. The loathsome spiders used as mounts by the Forest Goblins are easily able to traverse obstacles and rough territory. They are not slowed by difficult or very difficult terrain or obstacles.

Poisoned Attacks (Spiders only);
Fear Elves (see page 22);
Fast Cavalry

WYVERNS

Wyverns are vast, scaled beasts with broad wings and huge, fearsome jaws. Their hide is well armoured with bony scales and their tail drips with black venom that hisses when it touches the ground. They live in dark caves, high in the most barren of mountains in the Worlds Edge range. Occasionally Wyverns venture from their mountain top eyries and are seen flying over the plains below. This is universally seen as a bad omen by the weakling races of Men and Elves, though the greenskins greet them with whoops and cheers.

No Orc would be foolish enough to try and tame a fully grown Wyvern, but sometimes a well-bullied Gobbo can be threatened into stealing an egg or a new hatchling. These can be hand-reared to obey their masters (at least some of the time), and a trained Wyvern is the pride of the toughest Orc Warlords.

	M	WS	BS	S	T	W	I	A	Ld
Wyvern	4	5	0	6	5	5	3	3	6

SPECIAL RULES
**Large Target; Fly; Terror; Poisoned Attacks;
Scaly Skin (4+)**

GIANTS

Giants and greenskins have a long history of association and it is common to find that a greenskin horde includes a Giant brought along to add weight (and height) to the army's combat prowess. It's not altogether clear why greenies and Giants should get on so well, but it is noticeable that Giants are one of the few races that are considerably bigger and dimmer than even the biggest, thickest Orc.

To the greenskins, a Giant is a force of nature akin to a manifestation of their god, Gork (or possibly Mork). Such is the sheer destruction unleashed when a Giant charges that Orcs and Goblins are driven into a frenzy of gleeful cheering and whooping. To an Orc, there is no sight in the world so inspiring as a big, angry giant laying waste to their enemies.

For their part, Giants are more than happy to join a band of greenskins for the chance to eat people and get their hands on strong liquor. They're especially keen on the endless opportunities for thumping people. If the odd Goblin happens to get scoffed along the way no one seems to mind – this kind of thing is just part of the rough and tumble of existence when you're green.

	M	WS	BS	S	T	W	I	A	Ld
Giant	6	3	3	6	5	6	3	Special	10

SPECIAL RULES

Large Target; Terror; Stubborn

Longshanks: Giants have long limbs and move over normal obstacles such as walls, ditches and fences without breaking stride. Treat such obstacles as open ground when working out how far the Giant moves. However, when crossing such obstacles the player must test to see if the Giant falls over (see below).

Fall Over: Giants are ungainly and frequently befuddled, as a consequence of which they often fall down. They are especially prone to this if they've been raiding the local brewery.

A Giant must test to see whether it falls over if any of the following apply:

1) When it is beaten in close combat. Test once results are established but before taking a Break test.

2) If it is fleeing at the start of the movement phase.

3) When it crosses an obstacle. Test when the obstacle is reached.

4) If the Giant decides to Jump Up and Down on an enemy. Test immediately beforehand.

To see if the Giant falls over roll a D6. If is a 1, the Giant falls over. (A slain Giant falls over automatically.)

To determine in which direction the Giant falls, roll a scatter dice. Place the Fallen Giant template with its feet at the model's base and its head in the direction of the fall. Any models lying completely under the template are automatically hit. Any models partly covered are hit on a 4+.

A model hit by a falling Giant takes a Strength 6 hit causing D3 wounds. If the unit is in combat and the Giant has fallen over whilst attempting to Jump Up and Down, wounds inflicted by a falling Giant count towards the combat result.

A Giant that falls over automatically suffers 1 wound with no armour saves allowed. If the Giant is in combat then this wound counts towards combat resolution.

Once on the ground (you may lie the model down if you wish) a Giant may get up in his following movement phase, but may not move that turn. Whilst on the ground a Giant may not attack, but he can still defend himself after a fashion so the enemy must still roll to score hits on him. If forced to flee whilst on the ground the Giant is slain – the enemy swarm over him and cut him to pieces. If the Giant gets the opportunity to pursue his foes whilst he's on the ground he stands up instead. A Giant may attack on the turn it stands up.

Giant Special Attacks: Giants do not attack in the same way as other creatures though they select their victims as normal. They are far too large and fractious to take orders, and much too scatterbrained to have any sort of coherent plan. To determine what happens, each close combat phase roll a D6 on one of the following tables when it is the Giant's turn to fight. Which table you use depends on the size of the Giant's victim. When fighting characters riding monsters, decide whether to attack the rider or mount, as normal and use the appropriate table for the size of the target.

Giant fighting big things (Ogres, Kroxigors, Minotaurs or similar sized or larger creatures including chariots and war machines):

D6	Result
1	Yell and Bawl
2-4	Thump With Club
5-6	'Eadbutt

Giant fighting anyone smaller than above:

D6	Result
1	Yell and Bawl
2	Jump Up and Down
3	Pick Up and…
4-6	Swing With Club

Yell and Bawl: The Giant yells and bawls at the enemy. This is not pleasant as Giants are deafeningly loud and tend towards poor oral hygiene. Neither the Giant nor models in contact with him actually fight if they have not already done so this round. The Giant's side automatically wins the combat by 2 points.

Thump with Club: The Giant picks one model as his target and brings down his club with a single mighty strike. The target may attempt to avoid the blow by passing an Initiative test (use the lowest if the model has several different values). If the target is struck it takes 2D6 wounds with no armour save allowed. If a double is rolled the Giant's club embeds itself in the ground and the Giant cannot attack at all in the following round whilst he recovers his weapon.

'Eadbutt: The Giant head-butts his enemy, automatically inflicting 1 wound with no armour saves allowed. If the victim is wounded but not slain then he is dazed and loses all of his following attacks. If the target has not yet attacked that combat round he loses those Attacks, if he has already attacked he loses the following round's attacks.

Jump Up and Down: The Giant jumps up and down vigorously on top of one enemy unit in base contact. Before he starts, the Giant must test to determine if he falls over (see earlier). If he falls over, work out where he falls and calculate damage as already described. Any wounds caused by the fall (on either side) count towards the combat result. Assuming that he remains on his none too nimble feet, the Giant bounds up and down on the enemy unit, guffawing madly.

The unit sustains 2D6 Strength 6 hits allocated as shooting hits. Work out damage and saves as usual. Giants enjoy jumping up and down on their enemies so much that a Giant that does so in one combat round will automatically do so in the following round if he is able to, assuming that he did not fall over in the previous round. A Giant that starts to Jump Up and Down will therefore continue to do so until he falls over or until the combat comes to an end.

Pick Up and… : The Giant stoops down and selects a model (Giant player's choice) that is either in base contact or touching a model in base contact (Giants have a long reach). The target may make a single attack to try to fend off the Giant's clumsy hand. If this attack hits and wounds the Giant, the Giant's attack fails, otherwise the Giant grabs the model and the player rolls a D6 to see what happens next:

D6	Result
1	**Stuff into Bag.** The Giant stuffs the victim into his bag along with sheep, cows and other plunder. The model is effectively a casualty and can do nothing whilst in the bag, but if the Giant should be slain any enemy trapped in his bag are freed unharmed at the end of the battle. Victory points are not awarded to the enemy for freed models.
2	**Throw Back into Combat.** The victim is hurled back into his own unit like a living missile. This causes a wound on the victim with no saves of any kind allowed, and D6 Strength 3 hits (saves as normal) on the unit.
3	**Hurl.** The victim is hurled into any enemy unit within 12" of the Giant – randomly determine which. This causes a wound on the victim with no armour saves allowed, and D6 Strength 3 hits (saves as normal) on the unit. If no enemy units are in range, treat this as a *Throw Back into Combat* result instead.
4	**Squash.** This doesn't really bear thinking about. Suffice to say the model becomes a casualty and is removed from the game.
5	**Eat.** The Giant gobbles his victim up, swallowing him whole. The model is removed from the game.
6	**Pick Another.** The Giant hurriedly stuffs the victim into his bag or under his shirt (or down his trousers if they're really unlucky) and attempts to pick up another victim. The second victim makes a single attack (as above) to avoid being picked up. If the Giant rolls a succession of 6s it is possible for him to amass a collection of trapped foes in his pockets and bags (not to mention down his trousers). Trapped models are effectively casualties, exactly as explained in the *Stuff into Bag* result described above.

Swing with Club: The Giant swings his club across the enemy's ranks. The Giant inflicts D6 Strength 6 hits on the target unit, allocated as shooting hits.

TROLLS

Trolls are large and hideous creatures, bestial and foul with long gangling limbs and cold damp hides. The most unusual and perhaps best-known characteristic of Trolls is that their flesh is able to regrow almost as quickly as it is damaged. If a Troll's hand is severed, a fresh one will grow from the stump. The only thing that a Troll can't endure is fire. If they are burned they cannot regenerate, so fire is the greatest weapon for those in the unfortunate position of having to fight one.

Trolls will sometimes join Orcs and Goblins as they march to battle, although it is doubtful if they really understand what is going on. More often they simply latch on to passing tribes, attracted by the rotten carcasses, bones and refuse on which they like to feast.

	M	WS	BS	S	T	W	I	A	Ld
Troll	6	3	1	5	4	3	1	3	4

SPECIAL RULES
Fear; Stupidity; Regenerate

Troll Vomit. A unit of Trolls can make Vomit Attacks instead of ordinary attacks during close combat. Each Troll can make only 1 Vomit Attack at Strength 5, although these always hit and the corrosive, semi-liquid nature of Troll vomit allows no armour save.

Trollish Types. Trolls are liable to wide physical variation. All the models in a unit of Trolls are considered to be of the same type.

Stone Trolls. Stone Trolls have a tough, rocky hide and are all but immune to the effects of magic. They consequently have Magical Resistance (2) and scaly skin (5+).

River Trolls. Enemies attempting to attack a River Troll in close combat suffer a -1 penalty on their dice rolls to hit due to the stench and slime.

GORBAD IRONCLAW

In many records, Gorbad was the mightiest Orc Warlord that ever lived. Atop his fearsome (and explosively flatulent) boar, Gnarla, Gorbad drove his horde across the Empire, sacking and burning many great cities and even bringing Altdorf under siege. Even today, many centuries after his death, the name of Gorbad Ironclaw is feared in the Empire and his memory kept alive by the Orc Warlords that have succeeded him. Perhaps none will ever be as great again – he is the greatest of all Orc Warbosses and an inspiration to all Orc-kind.

Gorbad is an Orc Warboss. A warlord of incredible ability, Gorbad can incite his followers to great (and bloodily violent) deeds.

	M	WS	BS	S	T	W	I	A	Ld
Gorbad	4	7	3	5	5	3	5	4	10
Gnarla	7	3	0	4	4	1	3	1	3

Mount: Gorbad rides Gnarla – a huge war boar

Wargear: Morglor the Mangler and heavy armour.

SPECIAL RULES

Da Boss 'as a Plan. Gorbad acts as the general and battle standard of your army. You may not choose a separate battle standard bearer in an army that includes Gorbad. In addition, such is Gorbad's aura of Bossness that friendly units may use both the Battle Standard ability and his Leadership if they are within 18", rather than 12". However, if Gorbad suffers a wound, his ladz will quickly lose some of their confidence in him and the range of both abilities is reduced to 6".

Orcs are Da Best: Gorbad was the most inspirational Orc warleader of all time, and as such drew the biggest and best Orc fighters from all around to fight under his banner. As a consequence, any number of units of Orc Boyz and Orc Boar Boyz may be upgraded to Big 'Uns.

Thick-skinned. Gorbad receives an armour save bonus of +2 rather than the usual +1 for ordinary cavalry mounts, for a total save of 3+.

Tusker Charge. A charging boar is a bad-tempered mound of bloody-minded muscle with pointy tusks and bad attitude. Gnarla therefore receives +2 Strength during the turn in which he charges.

MAGIC ITEMS
MORGLOR THE MANGLER

Morglor the Mangler is one of the most feared weapons ever to be wielded by an Orc warlord, its thirst for mayhem and death matched only by that of its owner.

When using Morglor the Mangler, Gorbad always strikes first. No armour saves are possible against wounds caused by this weapon.

AZHAG THE SLAUGHTERER

One of the most dangerous Orc Warlords of recent history, Azhag's campaigns of destruction brought the eastern provinces of the Empire to the brink of ruin. Azhag possessed a strange iron crown, which appeared to give him sorcerous powers. Azhag rides to battle on the back of his malodorous Wyvern, Skullmuncha, directing the arcane fury of his crown against the foe.

Azhag is an Orc Warboss and is an excellent way to combine the brutal might of an Orc Warboss with the abilities of a Wizard.

	M	WS	BS	S	T	W	I	A	Ld
Azhag	4	7	3	5	5	3	5	4	9
Skullmuncha	4	5	0	6	5	5	3	3	6

Mount: Skullmuncha the Wyvern.

Wargear: Slagga's Slashas, Azhag's 'Ard Armour and the Crown of Sorcery.

SPECIAL RULES

Get on Wiv it!: A unit that rolls a 1 for an Animosity test within 6" of Azhag will ignore the result and immediately roll again. If this second roll is also a 1 then even the menacing presence of the Slaughterer cannot keep the greenskins in order.

Skullmuncha: As a Wyvern, Skullmuncha has the Large Target, Terror, Fly, Poisoned Attacks, and Scaly Skin (4+) special rules.

MAGIC ITEMS
SLAGGA'S SLASHAS

Azhag has carried these crude weapons for most of his violent career, and with them has cleaved both enemies and rivals.

The Slashas give Azhag +1 Attack. In addition, Azhag may re-roll any missed To Hit rolls in the first round of any combat.

AZHAG'S 'ARD AMOUR

The 'Ard Armour has saved Azhag's skin on many occasions, the many charms worked into it lending the iron supernatural hardness.

Heavy armour. The 'Ard Armour gives Azhag a 5+ ward save.

THE CROWN OF SORCERY

The Crown of Sorcery speaks to Azhag with a voice as dry as the grave and as old as the southern deserts, offering words of counsel and power way beyond the ken of most Orcs.

The whispering voices of the Crown provide all the knowledge required to cast spells. Azhag is a second level Wizard, who chooses spells from the Lore of Death. Having two voices in his head can get pretty confusing at times – for himself and his followers both. As a result, Azhag suffers from Stupidity.

THE BATTLE OF BUTCHER'S HILL

Azhag's reign of terror lasted for four years, and saw dozens of towns in the Empire's northern provinces razed to cinders. It was at the Battle of Butcher's Hill, however, that Azhag earned the title 'Slaughterer'.

The battle commenced with Azhag deploying his horde in three separate cohorts – an act unheard of amongst the notoriously direct and unsophisticated Orc Warlords. The first cohort, led by Azhag's Black Orcs and Big 'Uns engaged the defenders head on. The second commenced a wide sweep around the base of the hill, the great mass of Orcs and Goblins blocking the reinforcement of those facing the wrath of the Black Orcs. The third cohort, consisting of uncounted numbers of Goblins and Snotlings, outflanked the defenders. The nimble creatures climbed the hill's flanks and spilled around the defenders until they were entirely surrounded.

As if such a cunning deployment by an Orcish Warlord were not dire enough, what followed would serve to ensure Azhag a place amongst the most hated of Man's foes.

Bellowing in a voice not his own, Azhag drew on the sorcerous powers granted him by the ancient crown mounted upon his heavy brow. His words bound the spirits of the recently slain, and turned them upon their still-living fellows. The last, doomed defenders of Butcher's Hill stood back-to-back upon its craggy peak, battling Azhag's Orcs whilst the bloody limbs of recently killed brothers tore at them from below. So terrible was the slaughter that none escaped Butcher's Hill, the slain being bound to Azhag's will, enslaved and forced to rage bitter, resentful war upon their living kin.

GRIMGOR IRONHIDE

Grimgor Ironhide is, to many Orcs, the prophet and harbinger of Gork. He embodies the spirit of the wanton, bloodthirsty battle lust that drives every Orc. Armed with his magical axe, Gitsnik, and an unquenchable bloodlust, Grimgor has slaughtered his way across great swathes of territory, from the Blasted Wastes to the Worlds Edge Mountains.

Grimgor is a Black Orc Warboss. Truly da best fighter that the greenskin race has ever produced, Grimgor is an unstoppable killing machine, capable of turning an enemy regiment into a heap of offal.

	M	WS	BS	S	T	W	I	A	Ld
Grimgor	4	8	1	5	5	3	5	7	9

Wargear: Gitsnik and the Blood-forged Armour.

SPECIAL RULES
Immune to Psychology; Hates everybody

Da Immortulz: There must be a unit of Black Orcs in Grimgor's army. This unit of Black Orcs are as scarred and grizzled as Grimgor, veterans of his days in the wastes. The bodyguard is infamous for its standard bearer, Taugrek the Throttler, who recaptured Grimgor's personal banner when it fell in battle against the hordes of Vardek Crom.

Grimgor may only join this unit, and no other character may do so. If he does so, the bodyguard will be Immune to Psychology and will Hate everyone.

MAGIC ITEMS
GITSNIK
This large and blood spattered axe, whose name simply means 'foe killer', has many charms and pouches chained to its haft. These contain powerful sorceries woven by mighty Orc Shamans that enable Grimgor to wield Gitsnik with blurring speed.

This axe bestows +2 Strength. In addition, Grimgor always strikes first.

BLOOD-FORGED ARMOUR
Battered, scarred and twisted, just like its wearer, the Blood-forged Armour has served Grimgor well in many battles.

The Blood-forged Armour gives Grimgor a 1+ armour save and a 5+ ward save.

> *"I'm gonna stomp 'em to dust, I'm gonna grind their bones. I'm gonna burn down dere towns and cities. I'm gonna pile 'em up inna big fire and roast 'em. I'm gonna bash 'eads, break faces and jump up and down on da bits dat are left. An' den I'm gonna get really mean."*
>
> *Grimgor Ironhide, Black Orc Warboss*

GROM THE PAUNCH OF MISTY MOUNTAIN

Grom is a hugely obese and extremely fierce Goblin Warlord who ransacked not only the Empire, but the fabled realm of Ulthuan. According to legend, he once ate a plate of raw Troll meat, and this continues to regenerate within him all the time. As a result, he has developed an almost Trollish resistance to injury, but has also become very fat and suffers from constant agony and loud flatulence due to chronic indigestion. He rides a massive chariot, and swings the mighty axe Elf-Biter. He is accompanied at all times by his diminutive assistant Niblit.

Grom is a Goblin Warboss. Possessed of remarkable durability, Grom is an excellent choice to lead a Goblin horde to victory.

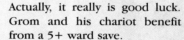

	M	WS	BS	S	T	W	I	A	Ld
Grom	4	5	3	4	4	3	4	4	8
Niblit	–	3	–	3	–	–	2	1	–
Chariot	–	–	–	5	4	3	–	–	–
Giant Wolf	9	3	–	3	–	–	3	1	–

Wargear: The Axe of Grom and light armour. Niblit carries the Lucky Banner.

Mount: A scythed Goblin Wolf Chariot pulled by three wolves. The combined model has a unit strength of 5.

SPECIAL RULES

Regenerate (Grom only)

Eats Elves for Breakfast: Having launched an invasion against Ulthuan, Grom has well and truly overcome his race's fear of Elves. If Grom is your general, all Goblin units in the army (including Grom) are exempt from the Fear Elves rule.

Niblit: Niblit is Grom's trusty battle standard bearer, and confers all the usual benefits. Niblit is

treated as part of the chariot model and although Niblit may attack, he may never be engaged separately, or issue or accept challenges. If the chariot is destroyed then Niblit and the banner will be lost along with it.

MAGIC ITEMS

THE AXE OF GROM

This large and forbidding axe is laden with barely contained Waaagh! energy, and its blows are inevitably fatal.

Great weapon. Attacks made with this axe benefit from the Killing Blow special ability. In addition, against any Elves, Grom's Axe will cause a Killing Blow on a 5+ instead of the normal 6.

LUCKY BANNER

Niblit carries this old and tattered banner to battle as a good luck charm. So far, it has not let Grom or his diminutive helper down.

Actually, it really is good luck. Grom and his chariot benefit from a 5+ ward save.

SKARSNIK, WARLORD OF THE EIGHT PEAKS

Skarsnik is the chieftain of the Crooked Moon tribe and the most powerful Night Goblin Warlord in the whole of the Worlds Edge Mountains. Skarsnik is infamous amongst the greenskin race for his astonishing sneakiness. He is remarkably cunning and is constantly luring his foes into ambushes and traps. He is always accompanied to battle by his enormous and voracious pet squig, Gobbla.

Skarsnik is a Night Goblin Warboss. Skarsnik is a daunting close combat opponent, and his Sneaky Scheming can put your opponent in disarray from the very start of the game.

	M	WS	BS	S	T	W	I	A	Ld
Skarsnik	4	5	3	4	4	6	5	4	8
Gobbla	–	5	–	6	–	–	4	4	–

Wargear: Skarsnik's Prodder and light armour.

Unit Strength: 3.

SPECIAL RULES

Fear Elves; Hate Dwarfs.

Gobbla the Cave Squig: Skarsnik's pet Cave Squig is a huge and disturbing sight, even to other Night Goblins. In battle, Skarsnik and Gobbla are treated as a single model occupying a single base. Should Skarsnik die, Gobbla is removed along with him.

Down in One: Gobbla's gullet is so deep and wide that he can easily swallow enemies whole. As such, Gobbla's attacks benefit from the Killing Blow rule – he does not stop chewing until his dinner is well and truly down, and is staying down.

Sneaky Schemes: Skarsnik is renowned for his evil sneakiness, sending his warriors through dank, secret tunnels to catch his enemy off guard before the battle has even been joined. At the start of the game, but before deployment, Skarsnik must roll a D6 for each enemy unit. On the roll of a 6, that unit has been delayed by a Wild Squig strike or some other such happening. Affected units do not deploy as normal, but instead enter the board from their deployment edge in the movement phase of their first turn exactly as if they had pursued an enemy off the board.

Tricksy Traps: Any Night Goblin unit that chooses to flee as a charge reaction and subsequently rallies at the beginning of their next turn may reform as normal, but is then also free to move during the remaining moves part of the movement phase. The unit is also free to shoot as normal (but it always counts as having moved).

MAGIC ITEMS

SKARSNIK'S PRODDER

Bound spell (power level 5)

This pointy implement is imbued with the bitter curses of Night Goblin Shamans and emanates the concentrated poison of their malice.

Halberd. The Prodder focusses the battlelust of surrounding greenskins and unleashes it in blasts of pure Waaagh! energy. It fires one blast each magic phase. The prodder's blast is a magic missile with a range of 24". It causes a single Strength 6 hit plus one additional hit for each unit of 10 or more Orcs, or 20 or more Goblins, within 12" of Skarsnik. No armour saves are allowed against this magic missile.

WAAAGH! MAGIC

Orc and Goblin Shamans don't use the normal lores of magic available to human Wizards. Instead they have their own brand of sorcery known as Waaagh! Magic. With typical Orcy simplicity, this is divided into spells of the Little Waaagh! and spells of the Big Waaagh!

Spells are chosen in the normal way, as detailed in the Warhammer rulebook. Goblin Shamans take spells of the Little Waaagh! Orc Shamans take spells from the Big Waaagh! table.

If a Shaman rolls a Miscast then he must roll a 2D6 on the special Waaagh! miscast table below.

WAAAGH! Miscast Table

2D6   Result

2   The Waaagh! power courses through the greenskin's tortured brain and explodes, unleashing roiling green energy. The caster is killed outright. Each model in base contact suffers 1 Strength 10 hit. All friendly units on the tabletop suffer D6 Strength 3 hits.

3-4   The caster's head disintegrates in an incandescent ball of Waaagh! energy and he is killed outright. Each model in base contact suffer 1 Strength 10 hit.

5-6   A malodorous cloud of green Waaagh! energy erupts from within the caster. He sustains D3 Strength 4 hits with no armour saves allowed.

7   The caster's mind is so befuddled by the dazzling Waaagh!ness of it all that he forgets the spell he was casting. He may not use that spell again in this battle.

8-9   Unable to channel the Waaagh! energy building within him, the caster inadvertently dissipates it within his own body – he takes a wound, with no armour saves allowed.

10-11   A sudden pulse of roiling Waaagh! energy shatters the caster's already tenuous grip on sanity. The caster is subject to Frenzy and Stupidity for the rest of the game – he may never lose his Frenzy.

12   In a dazzling display of green energy, the shaman inadvertently taps into more Waaagh! energy than he intended. The spell he attempted to cast is done so successfully, and counts as having been cast with irresistible force. The backlash, however, is spectacular – roll again on this table (re-rolling further results of 12).

THE POWER OF THE WAAAGH!

Where Orc and Goblin Shamans differ from ordinary Wizards is that their magical power is focussed by the mental energy generated by the greenskins around and about. Every Shaman can access energy through the Great Green, but localised energy makes a difference too. If the Orcs are fighting, a Shaman's powers are increased as he picks up the Orcish vibes from his comrades. This is normally a good thing, though it can be a bad thing if those vibes come from fleeing Orcs whose minds are panicked and confused.

1) If one or more Orc unit of twenty or more models is in combat at the start of the Orcs & Goblins player's magic phase, the Orc player may add an extra dice to his power pool.

2) If one or more Orc units of twenty or more models is fleeing at the start of the opponent's magic phase, the Orc player loses a dice from his dispel pool.

In both cases only Orc units are counted; Goblin minds are too weak to make an appreciable difference.

SPELLS OF THE LITTLE WAAAGH!

Goblin Shamans roll a D6 to randomly generate a spell from this chart. A Shaman can automatically swap one spell for *Gaze of Gork* if he does not generate it randomly.

D6	Spell	Casting Value
1	Gaze of Gork	5+
2	Brain Bursta	8+
3	Gork'll Fix It	8+
4	The Foot of Gork	9+
5	The Hand of Gork	9+
6	Mork Wants Ya!	10+

GAZE OF GORK
CAST ON 5+

The Gaze of Gork is a magic missile with a range of 18". If successfully cast, it hits its target and causes D6 Strength 2 hits with no armour save allowed.

BRAIN BURSTA
CASTS ON 8+

Brain Bursta is a magic missile with a range of 24". If successfully cast, it hits the target and causes 2D6 Strength 4 hits.

GORK'LL FIX IT
CAST ON 8+

The Shaman implores Gork to sow mischief amongst his enemies, inflicting a series of minor, yet distracting, calamities upon them. This spell may be cast on a single enemy unit (which may be in combat) within 24" and line of sight. Any of the unit's To Hit, To Wound, armour save or ward save rolls of 6 are counted as being 1s until the beginning of the next friendly magic phase. If an enemy Wizard is affected by this spell, any 6s in his casting rolls are counted as being 1s and can cause a Miscast and prevent irresistible force (in addition to any other effects).

THE FOOT OF GORK
CAST ON 9+

The almighty Foot of Gork stomps down on any one enemy unit on the table. The unit takes D6 Strength 6 hits.

THE HAND OF GORK
CAST ON 9+

You may cast this on one friendly unit within 24". If successfully cast that unit moves 2D6" towards the nearest enemy unit it can see – if it can see no enemy unit it moves 2D6" directly forwards. If this move takes it into contact with an enemy, it is counted as a charge – the moving unit need not take any Psychology tests that would normally be incurred for such a charge. An enemy unit charged in this way may only choose hold or flee as a charge reaction.

MORK WANTS YA!
CASTS ON 10+

The almighty Mork reaches down from the sky with a great green hand and seizes an unlucky foe, crushing them to paste between giant green fingers. Cast this on a single enemy model anywhere within 18" of the Shaman (line of sight is not required, even a model in a unit can be picked out, as can a character mounted on a monstrous steed or chariot). The victim must pass an Initiative test or suffer D6 Strength 10 hits.

SPELLS OF THE BIG WAAAGH!

Orc Shamans roll a D6 to randomly generate a spell from this chart. A Shaman can automatically swap one spell for *Gaze of Mork* if he does not generate it randomly. Spells that only affect Orcs affect all types of Orcs.

D6	Spell	Casting Value
1	Gaze of Mork	5+
2	'Eadbutt	6+
3	Bash 'em Ladz	6+
4	Fists of Gork	8+
5	Gork's Warpath	10+
6	Waaagh!	12+

GAZE OF MORK   CAST ON 5+

The Gaze of Mork is a magic missile with a range of 24". If successfully cast, it hits the target and causes D6 Strength 4 hits.

'EADBUTT   CAST ON 6+

Cast this on a single enemy model within 24" and line of sight (even a model in a unit can be picked out, as can a character mounted on a monstrous steed or chariot). If successfully cast, the 'Eadbutt causes 1 hit at a Strength of 5. No armour saves are allowed against the 'Eadbutt.

BASH 'EM LADZ   CAST ON 6+

Cast this on any one Orc unit that is in close combat within 18" of the Shaman. The unit strikes first in the next close combat phase and can re-roll any misses that phase.

FISTS OF GORK   CAST ON 8+

This has a range of 18" and may be cast on any single enemy unit, even if it is in close combat. If successfully cast, the unit is pummelled by a flurry of ghostly green fists. Every model in the unit takes a Strength 4 hit on the roll of a 4+ (roll for each model).

GORK'S WARPATH   CAST ON 10+

The almighty Gork goes on the warpath – his big warty feet stomping over the enemy army. Choose any enemy unit and stomp it as described for *The Foot of Gork*. After the first unit is hit, roll a dice and consult the following chart:

1   Gork slips and stomps on one of your units (your opponent chooses which). The spell ends.

2-4   Gork gets bored and wanders off. The spell ends.

5-6   He stomps another enemy unit of your choice. Roll again.

Units may only be stomped on once per successful casting.

WAAAGH!   CAST ON 12+

Each unbroken friendly unit immediately moves 2D6" towards the nearest enemy unit – if it can see no enemy unit it moves 2D6" directly forwards – war machine crew will abandon their machines. If this move takes it into contact with an enemy, it is counted as a charge – the moving unit need not take any Psychology tests that would normally be incurred for such a charge. An enemy unit charged in this way may only hold or flee as a charge reaction.

In addition, all friendly units strike first in the next phase of close combat and can re-roll any misses that phase.

SHINY STUFF

In this section the common magic items are listed first (see the Warhammer rulebook for a complete description). They are followed by a list of 'Orcs & Goblins only' magic items. These items can only be used by models from this book. Magic items must be selected within the points limitations set by the army list section. Note that all the rules for magic items in the Warhammer rulebook also apply to the 'Orcs & Goblins only' magic items.

Some items are restricted to a particular type of character, Night Goblins only, for example. Where this says 'Orcs' or 'Goblins' it includes all types of Orcs or all types of Goblin respectively.

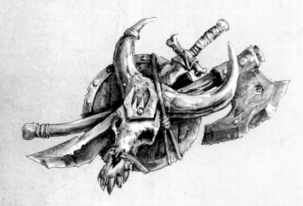

COMMON MAGIC ITEMS

SWORD OF STRIKING: 15 points
Weapon; +1 To Hit.

SWORD OF BATTLE: 15 points
Weapon; +1 Attack.

SWORD OF MIGHT: 10 points
Weapon; +1 Strength.

BITING BLADE: 5 points
Weapon; -1 armour save.

ENCHANTED SHIELD: 15 points
Armour; 5+ armour save.

TALISMAN OF PROTECTION: 15 points
Talisman; 6+ ward save.

DISPEL SCROLL: 25 points (one use only)
Arcane; Automatically dispel an enemy spell.

POWER STONE: 25 points (one use only)
Arcane; +2 dice to cast a spell.

STAFF OF SORCERY: 30 points
Arcane; +1 to dispel.

WAR BANNER: 25 points
Banner; +1 combat resolution.

MAGIC WEAPONS

WARBOSS IRONCLAW'S WAAAGH! CLEAVA — 100 points
Orcs only
One of thousands of blades from Gorbad Ironclaw's trophy pile, this sword has been 'improved' countless times by Orcish blacksmiths. At its core is a barely tarnished blade that will never lose its edge, as is the case with the most exquisite Dwarven craftsmanship.

All hits from this weapon wound automatically and allow no armour saves.

BATTLEAXE OF THE LAST WAAAGH! — 100 points
Orcs only
Revered subject of the Orc myth of the end of everything where Gork's (or possibly Mork's) chosen Best Boss Ragnar goes mad and destroys the whole world in an unstoppable orgy of fire and slaughter. This is foretold as the Day of Ragnarork.

The wielder of this weapon receives a bonus equal to his unit's rank bonus to both his Attacks and Strength – calculate this when the wielder makes his attacks.

BASHA'S BLOODAXE — 50 points
Orcs on foot only
Every Orc who has come to wield this axe has been overwhelmed with an incredible (and to Orcs, wholly admirable) bloodlust that can only be quenched by the wielder's death.

Grants +1 Strength in the first round of combat. The wielder of this weapon is subject to Frenzy. However, rather than receiving 1 additional attack for his Frenzy, the wielder receives D6 extra attacks. The wielder can never lose his Frenzy and may not join units (other Orcs are happiest to admire him from a distance).

SHAGA'S SCREAMIN' SWORD — 50 points
This blade has a curious enchantment that seems to empower the wielder in a manner proportional to the volume of insults he shouts at his foes.

The wielder of this sword receives +1 Strength and +1 Attack for each enemy character within 12".

SKULL WAND OF KALOTH — 40 points
Shamans only
Originally captured from the Necromancer Kaloth, this staff fascinated the Goblin Shaman Kazgi, who spent long hours attempting to plumb its secrets – until his mysterious disappearance.

For each successful hit inflicted by this weapon, the victim must pass a Leadership test (on its own, unmodified Leadership) or be slain instantly. No armour, ward or regeneration saves are allowed against this special attack. If the tests are passed, roll to wound as normal.

PORKO'S PIGSTIKKA — 40 points
Mounted models only

In battle, the gleaming point of the Pigstikka pierces enemy armour with ease, skewering several foes with one strike; "ready for later" as Porko used to say, referring to the traditional after-battle barbecue.

Spear. On the turn the wielder charges, he receives an additional attack for each point of rank bonus that the unit he is attacking has (up to a maximum of +3).

ULAG'S AKRIT AXE — 25 points

In battle this weapon writhes in the hands of the wielder, seemingly always having a shrewd idea of how best to strike the enemy.

The wielder may re-roll any missed to hit rolls. It also grants +1 Strength in the first round of combat.

BACKSTABBER'S BLADE — 25 points
Goblins only

Whilst Orcs are happy to fight anyone, anywhere, anywhen, Goblins are much happier if they can wait until their target is facing the other way.

Grants poisoned attacks. Grants the wielder +1 Strength if he is attacking the enemy in the flank and +2 Strength if he is attacking them in the rear.

WOLLOPA'S ONE HIT WUNDA — 15 points
Goblins only, one use only

Goblins still talk of the rebellious Wollopa, of his tremendous weapon and his even more awesome ability to outrun a galloping boar when he missed his target (which happened more often than not).

Once per game, this weapon grants the wielder Strength 10 for the duration of the combat phase. Use of the One Hit Wunda must be declared before the wielder makes any rolls to hit.

MARTOG'S BEST BASHA — 15 points

Old Warboss Martog the Mauler had a vast collection of weapons – most of which were stolen from other owners. His most favouritist of all was a massive Dwarven axe, heavy with runes and (since Martog's possession of it) Dwarven blood.

The wielder of this blade gains +1 Weapon Skill, +1 Strength and +1 Initiative.

SNEAKY SKEWERER — 10 points
Goblins only

Though crude enough to be readily recognisable as being born of Goblin craftsmanship, this sword has an unerring ability to find the vulnerable spot.

Wounds caused by this weapon suffer an additional -3 save modifier.

LUCKY'S DIRK — 5 points
Goblins only

An unusual magic is bound into this blade, growing stronger the more magical items there are nearby.

If the bearer strikes an enemy character carrying one or more magic items, his hits are at +1 Strength for each magic item.

MAGIC ARMOUR

ARMOUR OF GORK — 50 points

If armour is made with the correct rituals instead of just being bashed out of whatever bits of metal come to hand, it can be enchanted by a Shaman to offer a more formidable form of protection.

Light armour. The wearer has +1 Toughness.

SPITEFUL SHIELD — 25 points

This shield has razor-sharp teeth that snap and bite against unwary foes, making its bearer noticeably more dangerous and amused in equal measure.

Shield. Any foe that rolls a 1 when attempting to strike the bearer in close combat suffers a Strength 5 hit for each such roll.

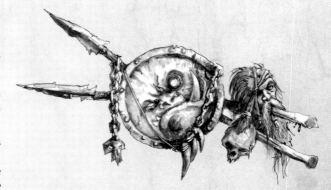

TALISMANS

EFFIGY OF MORK — 35 points

This ancient and slightly crumbly statue of Mork was formed from his own dung (or so it is said) in some distant age. Though it has undoubtably received several homegrown additions in more recent times.

All close combat attacks made against the bearer suffer -1 to hit.

WARBOSS UMM'S BEST BOSS 'AT — 30 points

This rune-encrusted and rather squashed looking helmet once belonged to a Dwarf king, or so legend tells.

Grants the wearer a 5+ ward save.

AMULET OF PROTECTYNESS — 25 points

The best form of attack is defence, and the best form of defence is the kind you can 'borrow' from your opponent, particularly if it's better than yours.

When the bearer of this amulet is wounded, he counts as having the same armour save and ward save as the model that caused the wounds.

THE COLLAR OF ZORGA — 5 points

This studded collar is inscribed with ancient glyphs entwined with the shapes of mysterious beasts. The wearer can stare imperiously at any beast that dares confront him and say "Don't even fink abart it!" or something like that, and the beast cowers before him.

Steeds, monsters (ridden and unridden) and beasts pulling chariots require 6s to hit the bearer.

ARCANE ITEMS

IDOL OF MORK   50 points
Orcs only

Mork loves nothing so much as seeing Orcs smashing their foes to the ground in a bloody mêlée. It is no surprise therefore that this Idol channels extra power to its bearer when the Waaagh! is breaking heads, and dissipates it when the greenskins are in retreat.

At the start of the controlling player's magic phase, the Idol of Gork adds one dice to the player's power pool for each Orc unit of twenty or more models in combat within 24" of the bearer. It removes one dice from the Orcs & Goblins player's power pool for each fleeing friendly unit of twenty or more models within 24"of the bearer.

STAFF OF SNEAKY STEALIN'   50 points
Goblins only

Goblins are well known for their ability to treat other people's property as their own and this generous trait even extends to magical power – as the seemingly Dwarven workmanship of this staff would attest.

At the start of each of your opponent's magic phases, you may take one dice from your opponent's power pool and add it to your dispel pool.

STAFF OF BADUUMM   40 points

Shaman Baduumm was a rebellious Savage Orc who dabbled in raw Waaagh! power more than was healthy for him. His charred staff retains an aura of power and an unlucky reputation.

Adds +1 to any casting attempts made by the bearer.

WAAAGH! PAINT   10 points
Orcs only

The crude Orc glyphs with which the Shaman has covered his body call upon the favour of Gork and Mork, but only bestow aid upon the Shaman when wetted with blood.

If the Shaman is in combat at the start of the Orcs & Goblins magic phase, he receives +2 to any casting attempts.

MAGIC MUSHROOMS   10 points
Night Goblins only, one use only

Most favoured of all mushrooms are those that grow in the deepest and darkest of caves and glow with an eerie green light. If consumed by a Shaman they can increase his oneness with the Great Green. They can also do something very nasty to his innards. Or both.

A single Magic Mushroom may be eaten to add D6 to the casting roll of a single spell. Decide after you have rolled your normal casting dice and add the D6 result to the total. However, if the 'Mushroom dice' is a 1 then the spell is miscast. A Shaman may carry any number of Magic Mushrooms, up to his maximum allowance for magic items. Buying one or more Magic Mushrooms does not count as taking an arcane item.

ENCHANTED ITEMS

THE HORN OF URGOK   40 points
Bound item, power level 5

If truth be known, most of Urgok's victories can be ascribed to the terrifying sound of this enchanted horn rather than his own generalship.

When this horn is sounded, all friendly units receive +1 Leadership (maximum of 10) and all enemy units suffer a -1 penalty to their Leadership until the end of the sounding player's turn. Roll a D6 after each use. On the roll of a 1, the bearer suffers a Strength 5 hit with no armour saves allowed as the power of the horn sounds the bearer instead of vice versa.

THE PIPES OF DOOM   35 points
Night Goblins only, one use only

A particularly fearsome set of squig-pipes, the ululating scream they emit when played can put cavalry to flight in a desperate attempt to escape the awful wail.

The pipes can be played at the start of the shooting phase. Each enemy cavalry unit, monster (ridden and unridden) and chariot within 24" must take a Panic test.

IRONBACK BOAR   35 points
Orcs only

A bizarre mechanical contraption created by Chaos Dwarf engineers, this boar weighs even more than its living cousins and is just as evil-tempered.

Boar. When charging, this steed does D3 Strength 5 impact hits in addition to its normal attacks.

WARBOSS IMBAD'S IRON GNASHAS   30 points

A huge metal jaw plate that belonged to the infamous Imbad. Such is the excessive bloodlust displayed by any Orc who dons this artefact, many believe that Imbad's psychotic spirit lives on within, urging the wearer on.

The character wearing the Gnashas gains the Killing Blow special ability in close combat. Chomp!

BIGGED'S KICKIN' BOOTS   30 points

Bigged, an old and boastful Orc, made his last boast in front of an Empire cannon. Only his boots were recovered – though his vengeful spirit (and the odour of his feet) lingers on.

Grants the wearer +1 Attack on his profile.

MAAD'S MAP   25 points
Models on foot only

A Goblin explorer without peer, Maad discovered many uncharted passes through the Worlds Edge Mountains – sometimes the same one several times in a single day.

Before deployment begins roll a D6. On 2-6 the bearer of the map may be deployed as a scout. On a roll of a 1, he got lost and must be deployed as normal.

TRICKSY TRINKET   25 points
Goblins only

If there's anything Goblins hate more than a fair fight, it's a fair fight where the other guy has some kind of magic wotnotz shielding him from a perfectly acceptable stab in the back.

Models in base contact with the bearer (friend or foe) may not take ward saves.

BRIMSTONE BAUBLE   25 points
Goblins only

Originally taken from the charred corpse of a Dark Elf corsair, this gemstone unleashes furious magical energy on anyone foolish enough to strike its bearer.

When the bearer is slain, all units (friend or foe) in base contact suffer D6 Strength 6 hits, distributed as for shooting. If the bearer is in close combat any wounds caused count towards combat resolution. If the bearer is fleeing, this item has no effect.

NIBBLA'S 'ITTY RING   20 points
Bound spell, power level 3

This crudely made gold ring has a huge green gemstone stuck to the top and glows even in full daylight. It is possible to harness the power within the ring to call upon the favour of Gork and Mork, but it is not always safe to do so…

The 'Itty Ring contains the *'Eadbutt* spell described in the spells of the Big Waaagh! Roll a D6 after each use. On the roll of a 1, the bearer suffers a Strength 5 hit with no armour saves allowed.

MAD CAP MUSHROOMS   20 points
Night Goblins only

Many kinds of fungus grow in the dark, dank caves of the Night Goblins, including the rare and treasured Mad Cap Mushrooms. Part of these form the deadly brew that sends the Fanatics wild, but only a small part. If they get a whole one each they go really mad.

If the character is with a unit of Night Goblins when their Fanatics are released he may give them each a Mad Cap Mushroom before they go whirling off. If they hit a unit (from either side) on the turn they are released they may re-roll the number of hits caused.

GUZZLA'S BATTLE BREW   15 points

Brewed with dangerously narcotic mushrooms and all manner of other, less identifiable, ingredients, this pungent liquid can rouse a greenskin to prodigious feats, or rot his innards into an unmentionable state.

The character with the brew is assumed to have 'bolstered' himself before the battle – roll a dice and consult the following table to determine the effects upon the drinker:

D6	Result
1-2	Subject to Stupidity for the remainder of the game
3-4	Hatred of all enemies for the remainder of the game
5-6	Hatred of all enemies and Frenzy for the remainder of the game

MAGIC STANDARDS

MORK'S SPIRIT-TOTEM   50 points
Orcs only

Mork's Spirit-Totem is a flag or, more often, a carved effigy of the great god Mork. Through the totem's eyes he watches over the greenskins and protects them from bad spirits, confounding the sorcery of enemy wizards.

This magical banner adds a number of dispel dice to the pool equal to the unit's rank bonus.

ROWDY GROTT'S BIG RED RAGGEDY BANNER   50 points
Goblins only

The big red raggedy banner belonged to the rabble rousing Rowdy Grott. Rowdy was an uppity Orc runtling who led a revolt of Goblins and Snotlings against his biggers and betters.

All Goblins within 12" of this banner may re-roll failed Panic tests.

BAD MOON ON A STICK   50 points
Night Goblins only

The ancient Bad Moon banner is tattered and stained, but is still much revered by the Night Goblins and fills them with bravery. Of a sort.

All Night Goblins in this unit are Stubborn.

THE SPIDER BANNER   50 points
Goblins only

Originally belonging to the Rootgrubbas Forest Goblin tribe, this banner appears to have been blessed by their fierce arachnid god, whom they revere alongside Gork and Mork.

All Goblins in this unit have poisoned attacks (shooting and combat).

GORK'S WAAAGH! BANNER   25 points
One use only

On the eve of battle the greenskin shamans invoke the spirit of the great god Gork before the tribe's mighty Waaagh! banner. The banner is liberally daubed with vast quantities of Orc dung, blood and spittle that will serve to absorb the battle-thirst of Gork.

The unit adds D6" to its charge move. Declare charges first and then roll. If the charge is failed, the unit will move forward its normal failed charge distance.

NOGG'S BANNER OF BUTCHERY   25 points
One use only

Nogg's notorious Banner of Butchery has been around so long it has absorbed a great deal of primal Orcishness as well as huge quantities of blood.

All models in the unit have +1 Attack in the turn the banner is used. In the case of mounted models, only the rider gets the bonus, not the mount.

ARMY LIST

This army list enables you to turn your Citadel miniatures collection into an army ready for a tabletop battle. As described in the Warhammer rulebook, the army list is divided into four sections: Characters (including Lords and Heroes), Core Units, Special Units and Rare Units.

CHOOSING AN ARMY

Every miniature in the Warhammer range has a points cost that reflects how effective it is in a battle. For example, a lowly Goblin costs just 3 points, while a mighty Orc Warboss will cost over 100 points!

Both players choose armies to the same agreed points total. You can spend less and will probably find it impossible to use up every last point. Most '2,000 point' armies, for example, will be something like 1,998 or 1,999 points.

To form your miniatures into an army, look up the relevant army list entry for the first troop type. This tells you the point cost to add each unit of models to your army and any options or upgrades the unit may have. Then select your next unit, calculate its points and so on until you reach the agreed points total. In addition to the points, there are a few other rules that govern which units you can include in your army, as detailed under Choosing Characters and Choosing Troops.

ARMY LIST ENTRIES

Profiles. The characteristic profiles for the model(s) in each unit are provided as a reminder. Where several profiles are required, these are also given even if they are optional.

Unit Sizes. Each entry specifies the minimum size for each unit, which is the smallest number of models needed to form that unit. In some cases units also have a maximum size.

Wargear. Each entry lists the standard weapons and armour for that unit type. The cost of these items is included in the basic points value. Additional or optional weapons and armour cost extra and are covered in the Options section of the unit entry.

Options. Many entries list different weapon, armour and equipment options, along with any additional points cost for giving them to the unit. This includes magic items and other upgrades for characters. It may also include the option to upgrade a unit member to a champion, standard bearer, etc. Orc and Goblin champions are referred to as a Boss.

Special Rules. Many troops have special rules that are fully described earlier in this book. The names of these rules are listed as a reminder.

CHOOSING CHARACTERS

Characters are divided into two categories: Lords and Heroes. The maximum number of characters an army can include is shown on the chart below. Of these, only a certain number can be Lords.

Army Points Value	Max. Total Characters	Max. Lords	Max. Heroes
Less than 2,000	3	0	3
2,000 or more	4	1	4
3,000 or more	6	2	6
4,000 or more	8	3	8
Each +1,000	+2	+1	+2

An army must always include at least one character to act as the general. If you include more than one, then the character with the highest Leadership value is the general. When one or more characters have the same (and highest) Leadership, choose one to be the general at the start of the battle. Make sure that your opponent knows which character is your general when you deploy your army.

CHOOSING TROOPS

The number of each type of unit allowed depends on the army's points value.

Army Points Value	Core Units	Special Units	Rare Units
Less than 2,000	2+	0-3	0-1
2,000 or more	3+	0-4	0-2
3,000 or more	4+	0-5	0-3
4,000 or more	5+	0-6	0-4
Each +1,000	+1 min	+0-1	+0-1

GORBAD IRONCLAW

Points: 310

	M	WS	BS	S	T	W	I	A	Ld
Gorbad	4	7	3	5	5	3	5	4	10
Gnarla	7	3	0	4	4	1	3	1	3

MOUNT: Gnarla.

WARGEAR: Morglor the Mangler & heavy armour.

SPECIAL RULES
Gorbad: Da Boss 'as a plan; Orcs are Da Best.
Gnarla: Thick-skinned, Tusker Charge.

AZHAG THE SLAUGHTERER

Points: 450

	M	WS	BS	S	T	W	I	A	Ld
Azhag	4	7	3	5	5	3	5	4	9
Skullmuncha	4	5	0	6	5	5	3	3	6

MOUNT: Skullmuncha

WARGEAR: Slagga's Slashas,
Azhag's 'Ard Armour and the Crown of Sorcery.

SPECIAL RULES
Azhag: Get on with it.
Skullmuncha: Large Target; Fly;
Terror; Poisoned Attacks; Scaly Skin (4+).

GRIMGOR IRONHIDE

Points: 375

	M	WS	BS	S	T	W	I	A	Ld
Grimgor	4	8	1	5	5	3	5	7	9

WARGEAR: Gitsnik and the Blood-forged Armour.

SPECIAL RULES: Immune to Psychology;
Hates Everybody; Da Immortulz.

GROM THE PAUNCH OF MISTY MOUNTAIN

Points: 255

	M	WS	BS	S	T	W	I	A	Ld
Grom	4	5	3	4	4	3	4	4	8
Niblit	–	3	–	3	–	–	2	1	–
Chariot	–	–	–	5	4	3	–	–	–
Giant Wolf	9	3	–	3	–	–	3	1	–

MOUNT: Goblin Chariot (armour save 5+).

WARGEAR
Grom: The Axe of Grom and light armour.
Niblit: Lucky Banner.

SPECIAL RULES
Regenerate (Grom only); Eats Elves for Breakfast; Niblit.

SKARSNIK, WARLORD OF THE EIGHT PEAKS

Points: 205

	M	WS	BS	S	T	W	I	A	Ld
Skarsnik	4	5	3	4	6	5	5	4	8
Gobbla	–	5	–	6	–	–	4	4	–

WARGEAR: Skarsnik's Prodder and light armour.
SPECIAL RULES
Skarsnik: Fear Elves; Hate Dwarfs; Sneaky Schemes, Tricksy Traps.
Gobbla: Gobbla the Cave Squig; Down in One.

ORC WARBOSS

Orc Warboss . . . . 120 points
Savage Orc Warboss. . . . . 125 points
Black Orc Warboss. . . . . 145 points

	M	WS	BS	S	T	W	I	A	Ld
Orc Warboss	4	6	3	5	5	3	4	4	9
Savage Orc Warboss	4	6	3	5	5	3	4	4	9
Black Orc Warboss	4	7	3	5	5	3	4	4	9

WARGEAR
Orc Warboss: Choppa.
Savage Orc Warboss: Choppa.
Black Orc Warboss: A huge array of choppas.

SPECIAL RULES
Savage Orc Warboss: Frenzy; Warpaint.
Black Orc Warboss: Quell Animosity; Armed to Da Teef.

OPTIONS
- Orcs and Savage Orcs may choose a great axe (+6 pts). If on foot may instead choose an additional choppa (+6 pts). If mounted may instead choose a spear (+3 pts).
- A Warboss may have light armour (+3 pts). A Black Orc may have heavy armour instead (+6 pts). Any Warboss may also carry a shield (+3 pts).
- May ride a Boar (+24 pts), a Wyvern (+200 pts), or may ride in an Orc Boar Chariot displacing one of the chariot's normal crew (80 pts).
- May choose magic items from the Common or Orcs & Goblins magic items lists, with a maximum total value of 100 pts.

ORC GREAT SHAMAN

Orc Great Shaman. . . . . 180 points
Savage Orc Great Shaman . . . . 185 points

	M	WS	BS	S	T	W	I	A	Ld
Orc Great Shaman	4	3	3	4	5	3	2	1	8
Savage Orc Gt Shaman	4	3	3	4	5	3	2	1	8

WARGEAR: Choppa.

SPECIAL RULES
Savage Orc Great Shaman:
Frenzy; Warpaint.

OPTIONS
- May ride a Boar (+24 pts), a Wyvern (+200 pts), or may instead choose to ride in an Orc Boar Chariot displacing one of the chariot's normal crew (80 pts).
- May choose magic items from the Common or Orcs & Goblins magic items lists, with a maximum total value of 100 pts.

MAGIC: The Great Shaman is a level 3 Wizard.
- May be upgraded to a level 4 Wizard for +35 pts.

GOBLIN WARBOSS

Goblin Warboss . . . . 65 points
Night Goblin Warboss . . . . 55 points

	M	WS	BS	S	T	W	I	A	Ld
Goblin Warboss	4	5	3	4	4	3	4	4	8
Night Goblin Warboss	4	5	3	4	4	3	5	4	7

WARGEAR: Hand weapon.

SPECIAL RULES
Fear Elves.
Night Goblin Warboss: Hate Dwarfs.

OPTIONS
- May choose a great axe (+6 pts). If on foot may instead choose an additional hand weapon (+6 pts). If mounted may instead choose a spear (+3 pts).
- May wear light armour (+3 pts), may also carry a shield (+3 pts).
- A Goblin Warboss may ride a Wolf (+18 pts), Gigantic Spider (+40 pts) or may ride in a Goblin Wolf Chariot, displacing one of the chariot's normal crew (+60 pts). A Night Goblin Warboss may ride a Great Cave Squig (+50 pts).
- May choose magic items from the Common or Orcs & Goblins magic items lists, with a maximum total value of 100 pts.

GOBLIN GREAT SHAMAN

Goblin Great Shaman . . . . 155 points
Night Goblin Great Shaman . . . . . . 150 points

	M	WS	BS	S	T	W	I	A	Ld
Goblin Great Shaman	4	2	3	3	4	3	2	1	7
Night Goblin Gt Shaman	4	2	3	3	4	3	3	1	6

WARGEAR: Hand weapon.

SPECIAL RULES
Fear Elves.
Night Goblin Great Shaman: Hate Dwarfs.

OPTIONS
- A Goblin Great Shaman may ride a Wolf (+18 points), or may ride in a Goblin Wolf Chariot, displacing one of the chariot's normal crew (+60 pts).
- May choose magic items from the Common or Orcs & Goblins magic items lists, with a maximum total value of 100 pts.

MAGIC: The Great Shaman is a level 3 Wizard.
- May be upgraded to a level 4 Wizard for +35 pts.

ORC BIG BOSS

Orc Big Boss . . . . 70 points
Savage Orc Big Boss . . . . 75 points
Black Orc Big Boss . . . . 85 points

	M	WS	BS	S	T	W	I	A	Ld
Orc Big Boss	4	5	3	4	5	2	3	3	8
Savage Orc Big Boss	4	5	3	4	5	2	3	3	8
Black Orc Big Boss	4	6	3	4	5	2	3	3	8

WARGEAR
Orc Big Boss: Choppa.

Savage Orc Big Boss: Choppa.

Black Orc Big Boss: A huge array of choppas.

SPECIAL RULES
Black Orc Big Boss: Quell Animosity; Armed to Da Teef.

Savage Orc Big Boss: Frenzy; Warpaint.

OPTIONS
- Orcs and Savage Orcs may choose a great axe (+4 pts). If on foot may instead choose an additional choppa (+4 pts). If mounted may instead choose a spear (+2 pts).
- A Big Boss may have light armour (+2 pts). A Black Orc may have heavy armour instead (+4 pts). Any Big Boss may also carry a shield (+2 pts).
- May ride a Boar (+16 pts), or may ride in an Orc Boar Chariot displacing one of the chariot's normal crew (80 pts).
- May choose magic items from the Common or Orcs & Goblins magic items lists, with a maximum total value of 50 pts.

BATTLE STANDARD BEARER
One Big Boss in the army may carry the Battle Standard for +25 pts.

The battle standard bearer cannot be the army's general even if he has the highest Leadership value in the army.

The battle standard bearer cannot choose any non-magical equipment except for light or heavy armour as appropriate. They may be mounted as normal.

The battle standard bearer can have any magic banner (no points limit), but if he carries a magic banner he cannot carry any other magic items.

ORC SHAMAN

Orc Shaman . . . . 65 points
Savage Orc Shaman . . . . 70 points

	M	WS	BS	S	T	W	I	A	Ld
Orc Shaman	4	3	3	3	4	2	2	1	7
Savage Orc Shaman	4	3	3	3	4	2	2	1	7

WARGEAR: Choppa.

SPECIAL RULES
Savage Orc Great Shaman: Frenzy; Warpaint.

OPTIONS
- May ride a Boar (+16 pts).
- May choose magic items from the Common or Orcs & Goblins magic items lists, with a maximum total value of 50 pts.

MAGIC: The Shaman is a level 1 Wizard.
- May be upgraded to a level 2 Wizard for +35 pts.

ORC & GOBLIN MOUNTS

	M	WS	BS	S	T	W	I	A	Ld
Wyvern	4	5	0	6	5	5	3	3	6
Gigantic Spider	7	3	0	4	4	3	4	3	7
Great Squig	3D6	4	0	5	4	3	3	3	3
Boar	7	3	0	3	4	1	3	1	3
Giant Wolf	9	3	0	3	3	1	3	1	3

SPECIAL RULES
Wyvern: Large Target; Terror; Scaly Skin 4+; Fly; Poisoned Attacks.

Gigantic Spider: Poisoned Attacks; Wall-crawlers.

Great Cave Squig: May not join units; Hate Dwarfs, Boiiing!

Boar: Thick-skinned; Tusker Charge.

GOBLIN BIG BOSS

Goblin Big Boss . . . . 35 points
Night Goblin Big Boss . . . . 30 points

	M	WS	BS	S	T	W	I	A	Ld
Goblin Big Boss	4	4	3	4	4	2	3	3	7
Night Goblin Big Boss	4	4	3	4	4	2	4	3	6

WARGEAR: Hand weapon.

SPECIAL RULES
Fear Elves.

Night Goblin Big Boss: Hate Dwarfs.

OPTIONS
- May choose a great axe (+4 pts). If on foot may instead choose an additional hand weapon (+4 pts). If mounted may instead choose a spear (+2 pts).
- May wear light armour (+2 pts), and may also carry a shield (+2 pts).

- A Goblin Big Boss may ride a Wolf (+12 pts), Gigantic Spider (+40 pts) or may ride in a Goblin Wolf Chariot, displacing one of the chariot's normal crew (+60 pts). A Night Goblin Big Boss may ride a Great Cave Squig (+50 pts).
- May choose magic items from the Common or Orcs & Goblins magic items lists, with a maximum total value of 50 pts.

BATTLE STANDARD BEARER
One Big Boss in the army may carry the Battle Standard for +25 pts.

The battle standard bearer cannot be the army's general even if he has the highest Leadership value in the army.

The battle standard bearer cannot choose any non-magical equipment except for light or heavy armour as appropriate. They may be mounted as normal.

The battle standard bearer can have any magic banner (no points limit), but if he carries a magic banner he cannot carry any other magic items.

GOBLIN SHAMAN

Goblin Shaman . . . . 55 points
Night Goblin Shaman . . . . 50 points

	M	WS	BS	S	T	W	I	A	Ld
Goblin Shaman	4	2	3	3	3	2	2	1	6
Night Goblin Shaman	4	2	3	3	3	2	3	1	5

WARGEAR
Hand weapon.

SPECIAL RULES
Fear Elves.

Night Goblin Shaman: Hate Dwarfs.

OPTIONS
- A Goblin Shaman may ride a Wolf (+12 pts), or may ride in a Goblin Wolf Chariot, displacing one of the chariot's normal crew (+60 pts).
- May choose magic items from the Common or Orcs & Goblins magic items lists, with a maximum total value of 50 pts.

MAGIC: The Shaman is a level 1 Wizard.
- May be upgraded to a level 2 Wizard for +35 pts.

CORE UNITS

ORC BOYZ

Points/model: 5 **Unit Size: 10+**

	M	WS	BS	S	T	W	I	A	Ld
Orc	4	3	3	3	4	1	2	1	7
Orc Big 'Un	4	4	3	4	4	1	2	1	7
Orc Boss	4	4	3	4	4	1	2	2	7

WARGEAR: Choppa & light armour.

OPTIONS
- Any unit may be equipped with one of the following weapons: additional choppa (+2 pts/model); spear (+1 pt/model).
- Any unit may be equipped with shields for +1 pt/model.
- Upgrade one Orc to a musician for +5 pts.
- Upgrade one Orc to a standard bearer for +10 pts.
- Promote one Orc to an Orc Boss for +15 pts.
- One unit in the army may be upgraded to Big 'Uns for +4 pts/model. A unit of Big 'Uns may carry a Magic Standard worth up to 50 pts.

ORC ARRER BOYZ

Points/model: 6 **Unit Size: 10+**

	M	WS	BS	S	T	W	I	A	Ld
Orc Arrer Boy	4	3	3	3	4	1	2	1	7
Orc Boss	4	4	3	4	4	1	2	2	7

WARGEAR: Light armour, choppa & bow.

OPTIONS
- Upgrade one Orc Arrer Boy to a musician for +5 pts.
- Upgrade one Orc Arrer Boy to a standard bearer for +10 pts.
- Promote one Orc Arrer Boy to an Orc Boss for +15 pts.

SAVAGE ORC BOYZ

Points/model: 8 **Unit Size: 10+**

	M	WS	BS	S	T	W	I	A	Ld
Savage Orc	4	3	3	3	4	1	2	1	7
Savage Orc Big 'Un	4	4	3	4	4	1	2	1	7
Savage Orc Boss	4	4	3	4	4	1	2	2	7

WARGEAR: Choppa.

SPECIAL RULES: Frenzy; Warpaint.

OPTIONS
- Any unit may be equipped with one of the following weapons: additional choppa (+2 pts/model); spear (+1 pt/model); bow (+2 pts/model).
- Any unit may be given shields for +1 pt/model.
- Upgrade one Savage Orc to a musician for +5 pts.
- Upgrade one Savage Orc to a standard bearer for +10 pts.
- Promote one Savage Orc to a Savage Orc Boss for +15 pts.
- One unit in the army may be upgraded to Big 'Uns for +4 pts/model.

GOBLINS

Points/model: 3 **Unit Size: 20+**

	M	WS	BS	S	T	W	I	A	Ld
Goblin	4	2	3	3	3	1	2	1	6
Goblin Boss	4	2	3	3	3	1	2	2	6

WARGEAR: Hand weapon & light armour.

SPECIAL RULES: Fear Elves.

OPTIONS
- Any unit may either be equipped with spears or short bows for +1 pt/model.
- Any unit may be equipped with shields for +1 pt/model.
- Upgrade one Goblin to a musician for +4 pts.
- Upgrade one Goblin to a standard bearer for +8 pts.
- Promote one Goblin to a Goblin Boss for +8 pts.

GOBLIN WOLF RIDERS

Points/model: 12 **Unit Size: 5+**

	M	WS	BS	S	T	W	I	A	Ld
Wolf Rider	4	2	3	3	3	1	2	1	6
Wolf Rider Boss	4	2	3	3	3	1	2	2	6
Giant Wolf	9	3	0	3	3	1	3	1	3

WARGEAR: Hand weapon & light armour.

SPECIAL RULES: Fast Cavalry; Fear Elves.

OPTIONS
- Any unit may be equipped with spears for +1 pt/model, and/or short bows for +1 pt/model.
- Any unit may be equipped with shields for +1 pt/model, but will no longer count as Fast Cavalry.
- Upgrade one Wolf Rider to a musician for +6 pts.
- Upgrade one Wolf Rider to a standard bearer for +12 pts.
- Promote one Wolf Rider to a Wolf Rider Boss for +12 pts.

FOREST GOBLIN SPIDER RIDERS

Points/model: 13 **Unit Size: 5+**

	M	WS	BS	S	T	W	I	A	Ld
Spider Rider	4	2	3	3	3	1	2	1	6
Spider Rider Boss	4	2	3	3	3	1	2	2	6
Giant Spider	7	3	0	3	3	1	4	1	2

WARGEAR: Hand weapon, spear & shield

SPECIAL RULES: Fast Cavalry; Poisoned Attacks (Spiders only); Wall-crawlers; Fear Elves.

OPTIONS
- Any unit may be equipped with short bows for +1 pt/model.
- Upgrade one Spider Rider to a musician for +6 pts.
- Upgrade one Spider Rider to a standard bearer for +12 pts.
- Promote one Spider Rider to a Spider Rider Boss for +12 pts.

NIGHT GOBLINS

Points/model: 3 **Unit Size: 20+**
(not including Fanatics)

	M	WS	BS	S	T	W	I	A	Ld
Night Goblin	4	2	3	3	3	1	3	1	5
Night Goblin Boss	4	2	3	3	3	1	3	2	5
Fanatic	2D6	–	–	5	3	1	3	D6	10

WARGEAR: Hand weapon & shield.

SPECIAL RULES: Hate Dwarfs; Fanatics; Netters; Fear Elves

OPTIONS
- Any unit may either be equipped with spears for +1 pt/model, or exchange their shields for short bows at no additional cost.
- Any unit may be equipped with nets for +35 pts.
- Upgrade one Night Goblin to a musician for +4 pts.
- Upgrade one Night Goblin to a standard bearer for +8 pts.
- Promote one Night Goblin to a Night Goblin Boss for +8 pts.
- Any unit may conceal up to 3 Fanatics (+25 pts/Fanatic).

SNOTLINGS*

Points/model: 20 **Unit Size: 2-20 bases**

*Snotlings **do not** count towards the minimum number of Core Units that you must include in your army.

	M	WS	BS	S	T	W	I	A	Ld
Snotling base	4	2	0	2	2	3	3	4	

WARGEAR
Sticks, rusty knives and rocks (hand weapons).

SPECIAL RULES
Immune to Psychology; Stubborn

SPECIAL UNITS

BLACK ORCS

Points/model: 13 **Unit Size: 5+**

	M	WS	BS	S	T	W	I	A	Ld
Black Orc	4	4	3	4	4	1	2	1	8
Black Orc Boss	4	5	3	4	4	1	2	2	8

WARGEAR: Heavy armour.

SPECIAL RULES: Armed to da Teef.

OPTIONS
- Any unit may be equipped with shields for +1 pt/model.
- Upgrade one Black Orc to a musician for +6 pts.
- Upgrade one Black Orc to a standard bearer for +12 pts.
- Promote one Black Orc to a Black Orc Boss for +20 pts.
- One unit may carry a Magic Standard worth up to 50 pts.

ORC BOAR BOYZ

Points/model: 22 **Unit Size: 5+**

	M	WS	BS	S	T	W	I	A	Ld
Boar Boy	4	3	3	3	4	1	2	1	7
Boar Boy Big 'Un	4	4	3	4	4	1	2	1	7
Boar Boy Boss	4	4	3	4	4	1	2	2	7
Boar	7	3	0	3	4	1	3	1	3

WARGEAR: Choppa, spear, light armour & shield.

SPECIAL RULES: Thick-skinned; Tusker Charge.

OPTIONS
- Upgrade one Boar Boy into a musician for +7 pts.
- Upgrade one Boar Boy into a standard bearer for +14 pts.
- Promote one Boar Boy to a Boar Boy Boss for +17 pts.
- One unit of Boar Boyz in the army may carry a Magic Standard worth up to 50 pts.
- One unit in the army may be upgraded to Big 'Uns for +8 pts/model.

SAVAGE ORC BOAR BOYZ

Points/model: 21 **Unit Size: 5+**

	M	WS	BS	S	T	W	I	A	Ld
Boar Boy	4	3	3	3	4	1	2	1	7
Boar Boy Big 'Un	4	4	3	4	4	1	2	1	7
Boar Boy Boss	4	4	3	4	4	1	2	2	7
Boar	7	3	0	3	4	1	3	1	3

WARGEAR: Choppa.

SPECIAL RULES: Thick-skinned; Tusker Charge; Frenzy; Warpaint.

OPTIONS
- Any unit may be equipped with spears for +2 pts/model and/or shields for +2 pts/model.
- Upgrade one Savage Orc Boar Boy into a musician for +7 pts.
- Upgrade one Savage Orc Boar Boy into a standard bearer for +14 pts.
- Promote one Savage Orc Boar Boy to a Savage Orc Boss for +17 pts.
- One unit of Savage Orc Boar Boyz in the army may carry a Magic Standard worth up to 50 pts.
- One unit in the army may be upgraded to Big 'Uns for +8 pts/models.

ORC BOAR CHARIOT

Points/model: 80 **Unit Size: 1**

Crew: 2 Orcs. **Drawn by: 2 Boars.**

	M	WS	BS	S	T	W	I	A	Ld
Chariot	–	–	–	5	5	4	–	–	–
Orc	–	3	–	3	–	–	2	1	7
Boar	7	3	–	3	–	–	3	1	–

ARMOUR SAVE: 4+

WARGEAR: The crew are equipped with choppas and spears. The chariot has scythed wheels.

SPECIAL RULES: Tusker Charge.

OPTIONS
- Any chariot may include an extra Orc crew model for +5 pts.

NIGHT GOBLIN SQUIG HOPPERS

Points/model: 15　　　　　　　　**Unit Size: 5-10**

	M	WS	BS	S	T	W	I	A	Ld
Squig Hopper	3D6	4	0	5	3	1	3	2	5

WARGEAR: Hand weapon.

SPECIAL RULES: Hate Dwarfs; Immune to Psychology; Skirmish; Boiiing!

NIGHT GOBLIN SQUIG HERD

Points/team: 30

	M	WS	BS	S	T	W	I	A	Ld
Night Goblin	4	2	3	3	3	1	3	1	5
Squig	4	4	0	5	3	1	3	2	3

WARGEAR: Hand weapon.

Unit Size: A Squig Herd is made of one or more hunting teams (a team consists of 2 Night Goblins and 3 Squigs). You can buy as many teams as you wish and add them together to form the unit.

SPECIAL RULES: Hate Dwarfs; Squig Herds; Wild Squigs; Immune to Psychology.

GOBLIN WOLF CHARIOT

Points/model: 60　　　　　　　　**Unit Size: 1**

Crew: 3 Goblins.　　　　　　　**Drawn by:** 2 Wolves.

	M	WS	BS	S	T	W	I	A	Ld
Chariot	–	–	–	5	4	3	–	–	–
Goblin	–	2	3	3	–	–	2	1	6
Giant Wolf	9	3	–	3	–	–	3	1	–

ARMOUR SAVE: 5+

WARGEAR: The crew are equipped with hand weapons, spears & short bows. The chariot has scythed wheels.

SPECIAL RULES: Fear Elves

OPTIONS
- Any chariot may include an extra Goblin crew model for +3 pts.
- Any chariot may include an extra Wolf to pull it for +3 pts.

GOBLIN ROCK LOBBER

Points/model: 70　　　　　　　　**Unit Size: 1**

Crew: 3 Goblins.

	M	WS	BS	S	T	W	I	A	Ld
Rock Lobber	–	–	–	–	7	3	–	–	–
Goblin	4	2	3	3	3	1	2	1	6
Orc Bully	4	3	3	3	4	1	2	1	7

WARGEAR: The crew are equipped with hand weapons.

SPECIAL RULES: Rock Lobber; Fear Elves

OPTIONS
- An Orc Bully may be added to any Rock Lobber unit to 'encourage' the Goblins for +5 pts. He counts as part of the crew. He carries a choppa, wears light armour and is an ordinary Orc.

GOBLIN SPEAR CHUKKA*

Points/model: 35　　　　　　　　**Unit Size: 1**

1-2 Goblin Spear Chukkas count as only 1 Special Unit choice

Crew: 3 Goblins.

	M	WS	BS	S	T	W	I	A	Ld
Spear Chukka	–	–	–	–	7	3	–	–	–
Goblin	4	2	3	3	3	1	2	1	6
Orc Bully	4	3	3	3	4	1	2	1	7

WARGEAR: The crew are equipped with hand weapons.

SPECIAL RULES: Spear Chukka; Fear Elves.

OPTIONS
- An Orc Bully may be added to any Spear Chukka unit to 'encourage' the Goblins for +5 pts. He counts as part of the crew. He carries a choppa, wears light armour and is an ordinary Orc.

RARE UNITS

TROLLS

Points/model: 40   **Unit Size: 1+**

	M	WS	BS	S	T	W	I	A	Ld
Troll	6	3	1	5	4	3	1	3	4

WARGEAR: Trolls don't need to carry normal weapons, though they often have a club, bone or bit of tree (these count as hand weapons).

SPECIAL RULES: Trollish Types; Fear; Stupidity; Troll Vomit; Regenerate.

OPTIONS
• Any Troll unit may be upgraded to a unit of either Stone Trolls or River Trolls at +20 pts/model.

GOBLIN DOOM DIVER CATAPULT

Points/model: 80   **Unit Size: 1**

Crew: 3 Goblins.

	M	WS	BS	S	T	W	I	A	Ld
Catapult	–	–	–	–	7	3	–	–	–
Goblin	4	2	3	3	3	1	2	1	6

WARGEAR: The crew are armed with hand weapons.

SPECIAL RULES: Doom Diver Catapult; Fear Elves.

SNOTLING PUMP WAGON*

Points/model: 40   **Unit Size: 1**

Note that 1-2 Snotling Pump Wagons count as only 1 Rare Unit choice.

Crew: Numerous Snotlings.

	M	WS	BS	S	T	W	I	A	Ld
Pump Wagon	2D6	–	–	4	4	3	–	–	–
Snotling crew	–	2	–	2	–	–	3	3	4

ARMOUR SAVE: 6+

WARGEAR: The crew are armed with hand weapons.

SPECIAL RULES: Oi! Pedal Faster; Stubborn; Immune to Psychology; Chariot; Crunch!

GIANT

Points/model: 205   **Unit Size: 1**

	M	WS	BS	S	T	W	I	A	Ld
Giant	6	3	3	6	5	6	3	Special	10

WARGEAR: A big club (hand weapon).

SPECIAL RULES: Large Target; Terror; Stubborn; Longshanks; Fall Over; Giant Special Attacks.

LORDS	M	WS	BS	S	T	W	I	A	Ld	Special Rules	
Azhag the Slaughterer	4	7	3	5	5	3	5	4	9	*Get on with it!*	p34
Skullmuncha	4	5	0	6	5	5	3	3	6	*Large Target, Fly, Terror, Poisoned Attacks, Sca...*	
Black Orc Warboss	4	7	3	5	5	3	4	4	9	*Quell Animosity, Armed to Da Teef*	p20
Goblin Great Shaman	4	2	3	3	4	3	2	1	7	*Fear Elves*	p22
Goblin Warboss	4	5	3	4	4	3	4	4	8	*Fear Elves*	p22
Gorbad Ironclaw	4	7	3	5	5	3	5	4	10	*Da Boss 'as a Plan, Orcs are Da Best*	p33
Gnarla	7	3	0	4	4	1	3	1	3	*Thick-skinned, Tusker Charge*	
Grimgor Ironhide	4	8	1	5	5	3	5	7	9	*Immune to Psychology, Hates Everybody, Da Immortulz*	p36
Grom	4	5	3	4	4	3	4	4	8	*Regenerate, Eats Elves for Breakfast, Niblit*	p37
Niblit	–	3	–	3	–	–	2	1	–		
Chariot	–	–	–	5	4	3	–	–	–		
Giant Wolf	9	3	–	3	–	–	3	1	–		
Night Goblin Great Shaman	4	2	3	3	4	3	3	1	6	*Fear Elves, Hate Dwarfs*	p24
Night Goblin Warboss	4	5	3	4	4	3	5	4	7	*Fear Elves, Hate Dwarfs*	p24
Orc Great Shaman	4	3	3	3	5	3	2	1	8	*Savage Orc Great Shaman has: Frenzy, Warpaint*	p18/21
Orc Warboss	4	6	3	5	5	3	4	4	9	*Savage Orc Warboss has: Frenzy, Warpaint*	p18/21
Skarsnik	4	5	3	4	4	6	5	4	8	*Fear Elves, Hate Dwarfs, Sneaky Schemes, Tricksy Traps*	p38
Gobbla	–	5	–	6	4	–	4	4	–	*Gobbla the Cave Squig, Down in One*	

HEROES	M	WS	BS	S	T	W	I	A	Ld	Special Rules	
Black Orc Big Boss	4	6	3	4	5	2	3	3	8	*Quell Animosity, Armed to Da Teef*	p20
Goblin Big Boss	4	4	3	4	4	2	3	3	7	*Fear Elves*	p22
Goblin Shaman	4	2	3	3	3	2	2	1	6	*Fear Elves*	p22
Night Goblin Big Boss	4	4	3	4	4	2	4	3	6	*Fear Elves, Hate Dwarfs*	p24
Night Goblin Shaman	4	2	3	3	3	2	3	1	5	*Fear Elves, Hate Dwarfs*	p24
Orc Big Boss	4	5	3	4	5	2	3	3	8	*Savage Orc Big Boss has: Frenzy, Warpaint*	p18/21
Orc Shaman	4	3	3	3	4	2	2	1	7	*Savage Orc Shaman has: Frenzy, Warpaint*	p18/21

UNITS	M	WS	BS	S	T	W	I	A	Ld	Special Rules	
Black Orc (Boss)	4	4(5)	3	4	4	1	2	1(2)	8	*Armed to da Teef*	p20
Fanatic	2D6	–	–	5	3	1	3	D6	10	*Fanatics (see Bestiary)*	p25
Giant	6	3	3	6	5	6	3	special	10	*Large Target, Terror, Longshanks, Fall Over, Giant Special Attacks, Stubborn*	p30
Goblin (Boss)	4	2	3	3	3	1	2	1(2)	6	*Fear Elves*	p22
Goblin Doom Diver Catapult	–	–	–	–	7	3	–	–	–	*Doom Diver Catapult, Fear Elves*	p27
Goblin Rock Lobber	–	–	–	–	7	3	–	–	–	*Rock Lobber, Fear Elves*	p27
Goblin Spear Chucka	–	–	–	–	7	3	–	–	–	*Spear Chukka, Fear Elves*	p27
Goblin Wolf Chariot	–	–	–	5	4	3	–	–	–	*Chariot*	p23
Goblin	–	2	3	3	–	–	2	1	6	*Fear Elves*	
Giant Wolf	9	3	–	3	–	–	3	1	–		
Goblin Wolf Riders (Boss)	4	2	3	3	3	1	2	1(2)	6	*Fast Cavalry, Fear Elves*	p23
Night Goblin (Boss)	4	2	3	3	3	1	3	1(2)	5	*Fear Elves, Hate Dwarfs, Netters*	p24
Orc (Boss)	4	3	3	3	4	1	2	1(2)	7	*Savage Orcs have: Frenzy, Warpaint*	p18
Orc Big 'Un	4	4	3	4	4	1	2	1	7	*Savage Orcs have: Frenzy, Warpaint*	p18
Orc Boar Chariot	–	–	–	5	5	4	–	–	–	*Chariot*	p19
Orc	4	3	3	3	4	1	2	1	7		
Boar	7	3	–	3	–	–	3	1	–	*Tusker Charge*	
Snotling base	4	2	0	2	2	3	3	3	4	*Immune to Psychology, Stubborn*	p28
Snotling Pump Wagon	2D6	–	–	4	4	3	–	–	–	*Oi! Pedal Faster, Chariot, Crunch! Stubborn, Immune to Psychology*	p28
Spider Rider (Boss)	4	2	3	3	3	1	2	1(2)	6	*Fear Elves, Fast Cavalry*	p29
Squig	4	4	0	5	3	1	3	2	3	*Squig Herds, Wild Squigs, Immune to Psychology, Hate Dwarfs*	p26
Squig Hopper	3D6	4	0	5	3	1	3	2	5	*Hate Dwarfs, Immune to Psychology, Skirmish, Boiing!*	p26
Troll	6	3	1	5	4	3	1	3	4	*Trollish Types, Fear, Stupidity, Troll Vomit, Regenerate*	p32

MOUNTS	M	WS	BS	S	T	W	I	A	Ld	Special Rules	
Boar	7	3	0	3	4	1	3	1	3	*Thick-skinned, Tusker Charge*	p19
Giant Spider	7	3	0	3	3	1	4	1	2	*Poisoned Attacks, Wall-crawlers*	p29
Giant Wolf	9	3	0	3	3	1	3	1	3		p23
Gigantic Spider	7	3	0	4	4	3	4	3	7	*Poisoned Attacks, Wall-crawlers*	p29
Great Cave Squig	3D6	4	0	5	4	3	3	3	3	*May Not Join Units, Boiing!*	p26
Wyvern	4	5	0	6	5	5	3	3	6	*Large Target, Fly, Terror, Poisoned Attacks, Scaly Skin (4+)*	p29

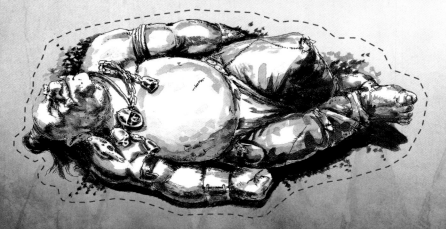

FALLEN GIANT TEMPLATE

To make your Fallen Giant Template, first photocopy this page and stick it to a piece of thin card (cereal packets are ideal).

Then, carefully cut around the dotted line with a sharp pair of scissors or a craft knife.

THE ORCS & GOBLINS ARMY

The following pages focus on the models that make up the Orcs & Goblins army. There are painted examples of the various characters and units, plus information about the banners and iconography of greenskin tribes that you can use to personalise your army.

ORC CHARACTERS

Warboss on Boar, with spear and shield

Warboss on Boar, with choppa and shield

Warboss with choppa and shield

Orc Warboss on Wyvern

*The captured
Crown of Solland*

Gorbad Ironclaw

*Gorbad's trophy
rack bears the
Solland Runefang*

Battle Standard Bearer on Boar

Orc Shaman on Boar

Orc Shaman

Orc Shaman

ORC BOYZ

Orc Boyz with choppas and shields

Orc Boy with spear
and shield

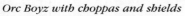

Orc Boy with
two choppas

Orc Arrer Boyz

Orc Warboss, Boyz and Shaman

BOAR BOYZ

Orc Boar Chariot

*Orc Boar Boy
Standard Bearer*

Orc Boar Boyz

Orc Shaman and Boar Boyz mob

BLACK ORCS

Black Orc regiment

Grimgor Ironhide

Black Orc Battle Standard Bearer

Black Orc Warboss with great weapon

Black Orc Warboss with two choppas

Black Orc Warboss with great weapon

SAVAGE ORCS

Savage Orc Shaman

Savage Orcs wear primitive garb made of animal skins.

Many Savage Orcs wear crudely daubed warpaint.

Savage Orc mob with additional choppas

Savage Orc Boar Boyz mob

GOBLINS

Goblin Shaman

*Goblin Warboss
with great weapon*

Goblin Shaman

*Goblin Warboss
with two hand weapons*

Goblin Shaman

Goblin mob armed with short bows

*Black and
white dags are
a common
motif in
Goblin tribes.*

Goblin with spear

Goblin Shaman and Goblin mob with spears and shields

Goblin Big Boss with spear, mounted on Wolf

Goblin Big Boss with hand weapon and shield, mounted on Wolf

Goblin Wolf Rider with bow

Goblin Wolf Rider mob with spears

Goblin Wolf Chariots

WAR MACHINES

Rock Lobber with Orc Bully and Goblin crew

Spear Chukka and Goblin crew

Goblin Doom Diver Catapult

FOREST GOBLIN SPIDER RIDERS

Forest Goblin Spider Rider mob

Spider Rider Standard Bearer

Spider Rider Boss

Spider Rider Boss

Some Giant Spiders are covered in vicious barbs.

Spider Rider Musician

Spider Rider Brave

NIGHT GOBLINS

Night Goblin Warboss with two hand weapons

Night Goblin Warboss with great weapon

Night Goblin Warboss with hand weapon and shield

Night Goblin Warboss with great weapon

Night Goblin Shamans

The Night Goblins unleash their Fanatics.

Night Goblins with spears, shields and nets

Night Goblin
Boss

Night Goblin with hand
weapon and shield

Night Goblin
with net

Night Goblin
Boss

Night Goblin
Big Boss

Night Goblins with bows

Night Goblin
Standard Bearer

Night Goblin Fanatics

Night Goblin Squig Herders

Squigs

Night Goblin Squig Hoppers

SNOTLINGS

Snotlings

The Pump Wagon is propelled by straining Snotlings.

A Snotling mimics the musician and standard bearer from an Orc Boyz mob.

Snotling Pump Wagon

SKARSNIK AND GOBBLA

Scalped Dwarf beards

Skarsnik, Warlord of the Eight Peaks and his pet Squig Gobbla

Skarsnik leads a Night Goblin mob against the Dwarfs.

TROLLS

Troll

Stone Troll

River Trolls

A Stone Troll mob

GIANT

ORC AND GOBLIN TRIBES

Orcs and Goblins are a ragtag bunch, and certainly not so organised as to wear uniforms. Despite this, certain colours and symbols serve to distinguish individual bands or tribes. Many players like to theme their mobs, or indeed entire army, to represent the warriors of a particular tribe. This page provides some example colour schemes, shields and banners – feel free to invent more!

Da Ironskinz tribe

Da Red Fang tribe

Da Splintered Bone tribe

Da Bloody Tusk Boar Boyz

This main colour of this unit of Red Sunz Orcs is red, signifying war in anyone's language.

Orcs are notoriously lacking in subtlety, and so the banner of the Broken Tooth tribe features a broken tooth!

The Skull Crag Goblins use a jagged white pattern to represent their cold home territory; this is further conveyed by the snow effect applied to their bases.

Da Dog Boyz

Moonjaw Forest Goblins

Creeping Death Forest Goblins

The distinctive flame designs on the hoods of these Night Goblins mark them out as Da Burnin' Face tribe. They also use the Bad Moon icon favoured by many tribes.

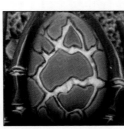

Scabby Eye Goblins

Forest Goblin of the Gloomfang tribe

Da Reavaz Goblin tribe

Da Crooked Moon Night Goblins

Da Bloody Sunz tribe

COLLECTING A GREENSKIN HORDE

This Orcs & Goblins army is a well-balanced force that will do well against any opponent. It has been chosen to a total of 2,000 points, a common size of army for Warhammer battles. The backbone of the army consists of mobs of Orc Boyz, Boar Boyz and Black Orcs. Augmented by the presence of the general and battle standard bearer these units pack a hefty punch that can crush most foes. The Giant and the war machines are there for anything the Core units cannot vanquish.

Orc Arrer Boyz
This is a unit of 10 Boyz with light armour, bows and choppas. It costs 60 points.

Forest Goblin Spider Riders
This is a unit of 10 Forest Goblin Spider Riders with hand weapons, spears and shields. The unit has a Boss, a standard bearer and a musician. It costs 160 points.

Orc Boyz
This is a unit of 16 Boyz with light armour, shields and choppas. The unit has a Boss, a standard bearer and a musician. It costs 126 points.

Black Orc regiment
This is a unit of 20 Black Orcs with heavy armour, shields, and lots of choppas. The unit has a Boss, a standard bearer and a musician. It costs 298 points.

Orc Boar Chariot
Costs 80 points.

Orc Boar Boyz
This is a unit of 6 Orc Boar Boyz with light armour, shields, spears and choppas. The unit has a Boss, a standard bearer and a musician. It costs 158 points

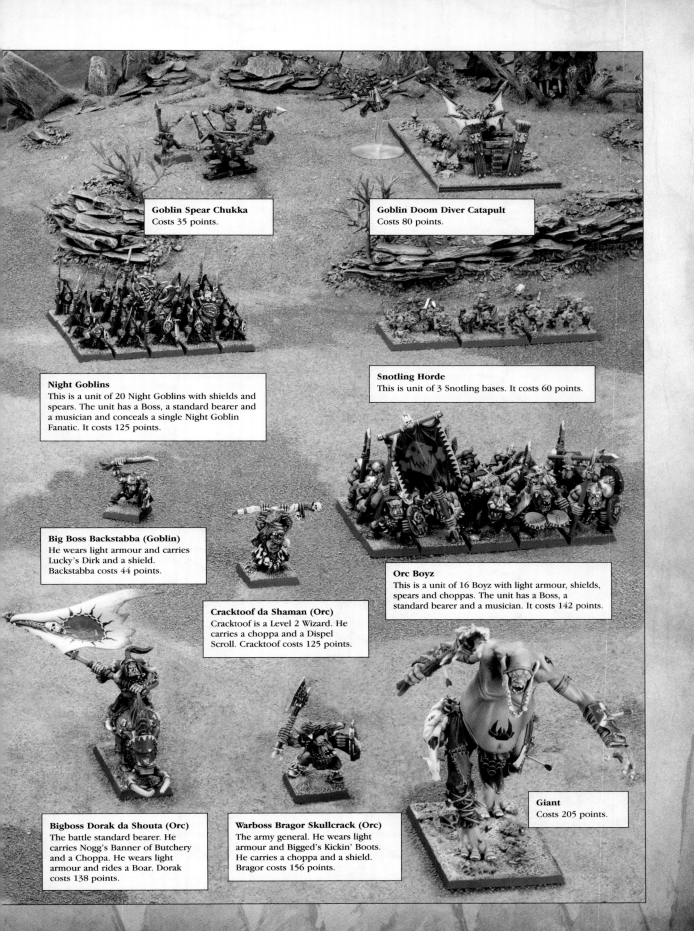

Goblin Spear Chukka
Costs 35 points.

Goblin Doom Diver Catapult
Costs 80 points.

Night Goblins
This is a unit of 20 Night Goblins with shields and spears. The unit has a Boss, a standard bearer and a musician and conceals a single Night Goblin Fanatic. It costs 125 points.

Snotling Horde
This is unit of 3 Snotling bases. It costs 60 points.

Big Boss Backstabba (Goblin)
He wears light armour and carries Lucky's Dirk and a shield. Backstabba costs 44 points.

Cracktoof da Shaman (Orc)
Cracktoof is a Level 2 Wizard. He carries a choppa and a Dispel Scroll. Cracktoof costs 125 points.

Orc Boyz
This is a unit of 16 Boyz with light armour, shields, spears and choppas. The unit has a Boss, a standard bearer and a musician. It costs 142 points.

Bigboss Dorak da Shouta (Orc)
The battle standard bearer. He carries Nogg's Banner of Butchery and a Choppa. He wears light armour and rides a Boar. Dorak costs 138 points.

Warboss Bragor Skullcrack (Orc)
The army general. He wears light armour and Bigged's Kickin' Boots. He carries a choppa and a shield. Bragor costs 156 points.

Giant
Costs 205 points.